MINISTRY

MINISTRY

A Theological,
Pastoral Handbook

Richard P. McBrien

1817

Harper & Row, Publishers, San Francisco

Cambridge, Hagerstown, New York, Philadelphia, Washington
London, Mexico City, São Paulo, Singapore, Sydney

FIRST EDITION

Library of Congress Cataloging-in-Publication Data

McBrien, Richard P.
  Ministry.

  Includes bibliographies.
    1. Pastoral theology—Catholic Church. 2. Catholic Church—Clergy. I. Title.
BX1913.M38 1987   253   86-43011
ISBN 0-06-065328-0

87 88 89 90 91 HC 10 9 8 7 6 5 4 3 2 1

To all who minister for the Church

CONTENTS

PREFACE

This is a book about ministry, but it is neither the first nor the last to be written on the subject. What makes this one different? Most books on ministry fall into one of two categories: either they present a *theology* of ministry, like the fine book by my colleague at Notre Dame, Thomas F. O'Meara, O.P., *Theology of Ministry* (New York: Paulist Press, 1983), or they offer guidance for the exercise of *particular* ministries, like Father William Belford's booklet, *Special Ministers of the Eucharist* (New York: Pueblo, 1979). There are many other good books in both categories. I single out these two only by way of example.

But not many books on ministry attempt to combine the theological with the pastorally practical. Those who are skilled in theology are often uncertain about pastoral matters, and those who are accomplished ministers at the parish or diocesan levels are usually hesitant to engage very much in theological reflection, at least in print.

I've tried to do both in this book—to offer a theology of ministry that is pastorally practical and to offer pastorally practical guidelines rooted in the best contemporary theology. For that reason I have subtitled the book *A theological, pastoral handbook.*

Who is the book for? For every minister of the Church, at every level: bishops, pastors, presbyters (ordained priests), deacons, pastoral associates, religious educators, church-school teachers and staff, youth ministers, hospital chaplains, eucharistic ministers, lectors, music ministers, ministers of hospitality, ministers to the elderly, ministers to the sick and the handicapped, college chaplains, social ministers, parish councilors, finance directors, family counselors, ministers to the separated and divorced, directors of communications, directors of ecumenical activities, directors of clergy education, seminary faculty and staff, directors of deacon programs, vocations directors, prison chaplains, diocesan newspaper editors and staff, and as many others as there are ministries in today's Church.

The book is intended, as well, for those now preparing for one of these ministries or who are simply contemplating the possibility. It is also a book for those responsible for identifying and recruiting good candidates for ministry, for educating, training, and spiritually forming future ministers, and for evaluating the pastoral performance of men and women already in ministry.

With that large and diverse readership in mind, I have deliberately written a short book. It will be left to those in various particular ministries to build upon the modest theological-pastoral foundation offered herein.

The first two chapters lay the theological and historical groundwork; the third and fourth make the pastoral and spiritual applications. In chapter 1, "What Is Ministry?," I offer basic definitions of ministry, of Church, and of the Kingdom of God, for which the Church exists and toward which all ministry is directed. Chapter 2, "How Has Ministry Evolved?," traces the history and changing views of ministry, from the New Testament to the present. It touches upon such issues as the relationships between clergy and laity, between bishops and presbyters, and between the power of orders and the power of jurisdiction. It also discusses the significance of ordination.

Chapter 3, "What Qualities Do Ministers Need?," offers seven basic criteria by which the Church can make responsible judgments about the qualifications and pastoral performance of its ministers. Those already in ministry can use these criteria as the basis for ongoing self-evaluation, and those who are preparing for ministry can use them as goals to achieve and standards to meet. Chapter 4, "What Is Ministerial Spirituality?," lays the foundation for a ministerial spirituality. It proposes ten criteria by which the active minister and ministerial candidate can discern among competing spiritualities. Since the whole book has to do with the *minister's* obligation toward the Church, there is a postscript on the *Church's* obligation toward its ministers. The relationship between the minister and the Church is reciprocal. Justice requires that the minister give his or her best effort in the service of the community of faith, but justice also requires that the community provide the minister with just and suitable conditions of service. The Church must practice what it preaches if it is to be a credible sign of Christ's presence to the world.

I have reproduced in an appendix the important pastoral

reflections of the United States Catholic bishops, *Called and Gifted: The American Catholic Laity,* commemorating the fifteenth anniversary of the Second Vatican Council's Decree on the Apostolate of the Laity. Many of the themes and principles articulated in that pastoral document are reinforced and developed in this book, especially the universal call to Christian maturity, holiness, community, and ministry.

There remains only my own obligation to express thanks where thanks are due: First, to Beverly M. Brazauskas, pastoral associate at Sacred Heart Parish, Notre Dame, Indiana, for reading the entire manuscript and offering many helpful suggestions for improvement. Second, to my colleagues in the department of theology at the University of Notre Dame who share with me the daily challenge of bridging the gap between theology and the needs of our ministerial students—in particular, Thomas F. O'Meara, O.P., Warren Professor of Theology and former director of the Master of Divinity Program; Robert Krieg, C.S.C., associate professor of theology and current M.Div. director, and Regina Coll, C.S.J., director of field education. Third, to those thousands of ministers throughout the United States and Canada who have allowed me over these past several years to test these ideas with them in lectures, workshops, conferences, and courses—especially my former colleagues and students at Boston College's Institute of Religious Education and Pastoral Ministry, which I directed from 1975 to 1980. Fourth, to my secretary, Donna Shearer, and my administrative assistant in the department of theology, Anne Fearing, for assisting in many ways in bringing this project to completion. And finally, to my editor at Harper & Row, Janice M. Johnson, who exhibited a saintly patience while waiting for the manuscript and whose fine editorial hand made this an even better book than it otherwise might have been.

Notre Dame, Indiana
June, 1987

Chapter 1

WHAT IS MINISTRY?

Before reading this chapter, scribble a definition of ministry on a piece of paper. The exercise will show that it's not so easy as it appears on the surface. Ministry encompasses a myriad of functions, but its whole is more than the sum of these functions. (If you write your definition now, you'll be able to check after finishing the chapter to see if it took everything important into account.)

Clear-cut definitions of ministry are indeed hard to find. In Bernard Cooke's major work, *Ministry to Word and Sacraments* (Philadelphia, PA: Fortress Press, 1976), which is more than six hundred double-columned pages, there is no definition of ministry. Instead there's a complete and detailed description of some of its functions: formation of community, proclamation of God's word, service to God's people, service to God's judgment, and celebration of the sacraments.

Edward Schillebeeckx, O.P., in his first book on the subject, *Ministry: Leadership in the Community of Jesus Christ* (New York: Crossroad/Continuum, 1981), also provided no explicit definition as such, although he occasionally came close. "Ministry in the church is not a status or state but a service, a function within the 'community of God' and therefore a 'gift of the Holy Spirit' " (p. 37). In a sequel, *The Church With a Human Face: A New and Expanded Theology of Ministry* (New York: Crossroad/Continuum, 1985), ministry comes to mean for Schillebeeckx both "the specific crystallization of a universal charisma of the spirit" and "a gift of the Spirit reserved for certain Christians with a function in the church" (p. 81).

Although Father Schillebeeckx has not given us a useful definition, he has made two important points: (1) ministry is both universal and particular, and (2) ministry is a function, not a state. Both distinctions are crucial—the second even more so than the first. One doesn't become a minister to *become* a minister, that is, to enter the ministerial state. One becomes a minister to *do* ministry, that is, to fulfill the function of a minister.

This is not to say that external activity is more important than internal, or spiritual, dispositions. Of course, one must *be* an authentic Christian before one can effectively *do* Christian ministry. The more authentically Christian one is, the more effective one's ministry.

Yves Congar, O.P., perhaps this century's greatest ecclesiologist, speaks of various *levels* of ministry. He suggests that there are three levels. The first is general ministry, rooted in the gifts of the Holy Spirit and expressed in various occasional, spontaneous, and passing services—for example, parents catechizing their children, a married couple giving advice to others who might be having difficulty in marriage, individuals visiting the sick and imprisoned or leading Bible study groups. The second is publicly recognized ministries more directly related to the needs and habitual activities of the Church—for example, permanent catechists, lectors, eucharistic ministers, choir directors. And the third level is ordained ministries, which are, for Congar, public offices whose base is sacramental—for example, diaconate, presbyterate, and episcopate.

Yet another Dominican theologian (and a colleague of mine at the University of Notre Dame), Father Thomas F. O'Meara, offers a readily discoverable definition in his book, *Theology of Ministry* (New York: Paulist Press, 1983). Christian ministry *"is the public activity of a baptized follower of Jesus Christ flowing from the Spirit's charism and an individual personality on behalf of a Christian community to witness to, serve and realize the kingdom of God"* (p. 142).

Ministry, according to Father O'Meara, has six characteristics: (1) doing something; (2) for the advent of the kingdom; (3) in public; (4) on behalf of a Christian community; (5) which is a gift received in faith, baptism, and ordination; and (6) which is an activity with its own limits and identity within a diversity of ministerial actions (*Theology of Ministry*, p. 136).

These attempts at definition by important Catholic theologians overlap in significant ways with similar efforts by theologians of other Christian traditions and by various ecumenical consultations. The Lutheran-Catholic dialogue in the United States, for example, makes a distinction between lowercase and uppercase ministry. Ministry with a lowercase *m* belongs to every baptized Christian and involves the task of proclaiming the gospel to all, believers and nonbelievers alike. Each of us shares in this ministry insofar as we belong to the priestly people that is the Church. Ministry (with a capital *M*) is a particular form of service within and for the sake of the Church in its mission to the world. It is a ministry of proclaiming the gospel, celebrating the sacraments, caring for the faithful, witnessing, and serving. It stands with the People of God under Christ but also speaks in Christ's name *to* his people. (See the suggested readings at the end of this chapter for information on *Lutherans and Catholics in Dialogue: Eucharist and Ministry*.)

The so-called Lima statement, *Baptism, Eucharist and Ministry* (Faith and Order Paper No. 111, World Council of Churches, 1982), makes a similar distinction between a general ministry, which is rooted in the gifts of the Holy Spirit and bestowed on every member of the Church, and ordained ministry, about which there is, of course, disagreement. According to the Lima document, the word *ministry* in its broadest sense "denotes the service to which the whole people of God is called, whether as individuals, as a total community, or as the universal Church." The words *ministry* or *ministries* "can also denote the particular institutional forms which this service may take" (II, 7, b, p. 21). The term *ordained ministry*, on the other hand, "refers to persons who have received a charism and whom the church appoints for service by ordination through the invocation of the Spirit and the laying on of hands" (II, 7, c, p. 21).

What should be clear from the overlapping definitions, which use different words to mean the same thing and use the same words to define different functions, is the lack of any unanimity about the nature of ministry. But that should not be surprising. Ministry has only recently become the subject of serious and sustained theological attention. It is remarkable that there has been so much progress in the last decade alone.

These are the constants we find in the various sources cited previously: (1) ministry is rooted in the Holy Spirit; (2) there is a distinction between general and particular ministry; (3) all ministry is functional, that is, for the benefit of others, not primarily for the benefit of the minister; and (4) ultimately all ministry is for the sake of the Kingdom of God, which is the object of the Church's mission. (I'll define what I mean by Church and Kingdom later in this chapter.)

TOWARD A DEFINITION OF MINISTRY

In light of this discussion and in light also of broader developments in the theology of the Church, or *ecclesiology*, I shall now propose a working definition of ministry that can prove useful to everyone involved in the recruitment, formation, selection, and evaluation of ministers as well as to all those already engaged in some form of ministry.

Like Father Congar, I distinguish among various levels, although there are some differences between the two approaches:

1. *General/universal ministry* is any service (which is the root meaning of the word *ministry*) rendered to another person or group of people who happen to be in need of that service. The call to ministry in this first sense is rooted in our common *humanity*. In other words, every human being is called to general/universal ministry. In this sense ministry has nothing intrinsically to do with religion. Examples of

this ministry include taking care of a single parent's children, shopping for an elderly neighbor, demonstrating against nuclear weapons, or contributing to a fund for starving people.

2. *General/specific ministry* is any special service rendered by people specifically called to serve others in the so-called helping professions and other service occupations such as nursing, social work, and legal aid. Their ministry is rooted not only in their humanity but also in a particular *competence* that is publicly certified or validated in one way or another, such as by licensing.

3. *Christian/universal ministry* is any general service rendered to others *in Christ and because of Christ*. The call to ministry in this third sense is rooted in our *baptism and confirmation*. Accordingly every member of the Church is called to ministry in this sense. And, in fact, when Christians perform the services in general/universal ministry, their actions are Christian/universal if performed out of explicitly Christian motives.

4. *Christian/specific ministry* is any general service rendered to others in Christ and because of Christ *in the name of the Church and for the sake of helping the Church fulfill its mission.* The call to ministry in this fourth and most specific sense is rooted in some form or act of *designation* by the Church itself. Thus it is sometimes called *designated at ministry*. Relatively few members of the Church are called to ministry in this sense.

A Christian who visits the sick on his or her own initiative is engaging in Christian/universal ministry. A Christian who visits the sick as part of a parish team that has been designated for this service is engaging in Christian/specific ministry. Other examples of Christian/specific ministers include directors of religious education, eucharistic ministers, lectors, ministers of hospitality, deacons, and, of course, bishops and presbyters.

With the declining numbers of vocations to the ordained priesthood in recent years, this ministerial category has expanded to include many lay people who were at one time excluded from meaningful participation in the liturgical, educational, administrative, and social ministries of the Church. But even if there had been no shortage of presbyteral vocations, this expansion would have occurred as a result of the Second Vatican Council's emphasis on the Church as the People of God (Dogmatic Constitution on the Church, chapter 2) and on baptism and confirmation as the sacramental foundation of Christian mission (Dogmatic Constitution on the Church, n. 33).

Of course, what ultimately grounds each of these four levels of ministry is the gracious action of the Holy Spirit. Each of us, Christian or not, ordained or not, is empowered by God, the author and source of all life and of all gifts, to do good for others, that is, to render unselfish service to our neighbors. The empowering, charism-bestowing God we call the Holy Spirit.

And every level of ministry in turn is oriented to the same reality—namely, the coming Kingdom of God, a kingdom not only of holiness and grace, but of justice, love, and peace (from the Preface for the feast of Christ the King, cited by Vatican II, Pastoral Constitution on the Church in the Modern World, n. 43).

When we're talking about ministry, therefore, we have to make clear just what level of ministry we're referring to. In this chapter and throughout the book, I am referring to ministry in all four senses, but particularly at the fourth level, designated Christian ministry, ordained and nonordained alike.

MINISTRY AND CHURCH

Ministry is difficult to define and individual ministries are difficult to distinguish from each other because ministry's origin and history are very complex. But there are some constants, one of which is that ministry is for the sake of the Church's mission. To understand Christian ministry (in its universal and specific meanings) one must see it always in relation to the nature and mission of the Church.

First, what do we mean by Church? (You might want to try your hand at defining it, just as you tried to define ministry.) Is the Church the hierarchy (pope and bishops) or is it the whole People of God? Is it the institution or is it the community? It's both, as a matter of fact.

Is the Church a parish, a diocese, or a base community, or is it universal and centered, for Catholics, in the Vatican? Is the Church local or is it international? Again, it's both. Finally, is the Church Catholic or Protestant? Is it Anglican or Orthodox? Is it denominational or ecumenical? One more time: it's both.

Thus, when we define ministry as a service designated by the Church for the sake of the mission of the Church, we have to be clear about the Church we have in mind. At the very least we have to be careful not to *exclude* any legitimate meanings of the word *Church*.

If the Church is not limited to the Vatican, then it is possible to have authentic, designated ministries that are not explicitly validated by the pope. And if the Church is not limited to the Catholic Church, then it is possible to have authentic, designated ministries in other Christian churches. And if the Church is not limited to the hierarchy, then it is possible to have authentic, designated ministries that do not appear in the local diocesan directory.

The word *Church* admits of many different, but not contradictory, meanings. Its root meaning is *assembly*. For our purposes here I define the Church as the whole community (assembly) of baptized persons called by God the Father to acknowledge the lordship of Jesus, the Son of God, in word, in worship, in witness, and in service and, through the power of the Holy Spirit, to share in Jesus' historic mission for the sake of the Kingdom of God. In short, the Church is the Body of Christ.

The Mission of the Church

The Church is first called and then *sent*. In other words, the Church is a community, or an assembly, with a *mission*. The mission of the Church is similar to that of Jesus Christ himself. Like Christ, the Church "receives the mission to proclaim and to establish among all peoples the kingdom of Christ and of God" (Vatican II, Dogmatic Constitution on the Church, n. 5; all Vatican II quotes are from the Abbott-Gallagher edition, *The Documents of Vatican II*, New York: Guild Press, America Press, Association Press, 1966).

First, the Church is sent to proclaim the Kingdom of God by *word*, that is, in preaching, teaching, and catechesis. Second, the Church is sent to participate in Christ's *worship* of the Father, in and through the power of the Holy Spirit. The Church does this especially in the Eucharist, which Vatican II called the summit and the source of the whole Christian life (Constitution on the Sacred Liturgy, n. 10) and which anticipates the feasting we hope to enjoy in the heavenly kingdom. The Church also celebrates and anticipates the coming kingdom in the other sacraments and in its general prayer life.

Third, the Church is sent to offer *witness* to the world of what it proclaims and celebrates. Because the Church is a sacrament—as Pope Paul VI said, a "reality imbued with the hidden presence of God"—it has to practice what it preaches. It is not enough that it *be* the Body of Christ; it must *look* and *act* like the Body of Christ. It is not enough that it *be* "the initial budding forth of the kingdom" (Vatican II, Dogmatic Constitution on the Church, n. 5); it must *look* and *act* like a community permeated with God's saving presence.

Finally, the Church is sent to provide *service* to those in need, both inside and outside the Church. In this regard it must follow the example of the Lord himself who, as the Suffering Servant of God, ministered to the sick, the poor, the handicapped, the oppressed, the socially ostracized, the sinners, and the dying. The Kingdom of God, after all, is a kingdom of justice and peace, as well as of holiness and grace.

"Action on behalf of justice and participation in the

transformation of the world," the Third International Synod of Bishops declared in its *Justice in the World* (1971), "fully appear to us as a constitutive dimension of the preaching of the Gospel, or, in other words, of the Church's mission for the redemption of the human race and its liberation from every oppressive situation" (para. 6).

Ministry is exercised, therefore, across the whole missionary spectrum. Thus there are ministries of the word (catechist, preacher), ministries of worship (choir director, eucharistic minister, lector, presider), ministries of witness (those that serve the ongoing renewal and reform of religious communities, of local churches, or of the universal Church), and ministries of service (social ministries of various kinds, such as to the elderly, handicapped, sick, and refugees).

Because the mission of the Church is not limited to liturgy, for example, there are more authentic, designated ministries than those related directly to the Eucharist and the other sacraments. And because service (*diakonia*) is part of the essential mission of the Church, ministries that serve the handicapped, the poor, and the politically oppressed are as authentic as ministries of preaching, teaching, and catechesis.

The Kingdom of God

According to Vatican II, "the Church has a single intention: that God's kingdom may come" (Pastoral Constitution on the Church in the Modern World, n. 45). This is not surprising since the Church is the Body of Christ and the Kingdom of God was at the very center of Jesus' own mission:

"This is the time of fulfillment. The kingdom of God is at hand. Repent, and believe in the gospel" (Mark 1:15).

The Kingdom of God, however, is harder to define than is the Church. You can see the Church; you can't see the Kingdom. Although the Christian believes that God is present and active in the Church, there is more to the Church than its divine and supernatural character. There is a human and worldly dimension that is within the reach, so to speak, of social scientists and other interested observers. People identify themselves and are identified by others as members of the Church. The Church has a membership list, owns property, has employees, registers with the government for tax purposes, and the like.

Accordingly, a sociologist can analyze the Church, examining its methods of recruitment, formation, and guidance, noting how power is distributed and exercised, measuring its stated goals against its palpable achievements. But a sociologist cannot analyze the Kingdom of God. The Kingdom of God isn't an organization, an institution, or a social movement. People don't "join" the Kingdom. The Kingdom doesn't own property, nor does it have any employees.

This is not to suggest that there is something unreal or abstract about the Kingdom. For the Christian the Church is always subordinate to the Kingdom. Whatever the Church is and does is always for the sake of the Kingdom of God.

What, then, is the Kingdom of God? A *kingdom* is a territory or region under a particular person's control. Thus we have the Hashemite kingdom of Jordan, under the control of the King of Jordan. His will determines social, economic, and political policy in Jordan. What happens in Jordan ultimately depends on the will of its king.

But *kingdom* can also describe a territory or region in a different, nonpolitical sense. A person is hired as a new secretary in a large corporation. As she begins her first day on the job, some of the other secretaries help to familiarize her not only with her duties but also with the politics of the office. "That one over there, the tall blond woman with the red blouse. She's a great person. You'd never know she's the comptroller. Very down-to-earth." Then the finger points in another direction. "But don't stick your nose over there. That's the executive vice-president's secretary. She runs that operation like a staff sergeant. That's her kingdom, and you'd better not forget it."

The Kingdom of God is more like the second than the first, but without the negative overtones. The Kingdom exists wherever and whenever the will of God is operative, wherever and whenever the will of God is fulfilled.

The Kingdom of God is as broad and as overarching as the will of God is broad and overarching. In God, of course, everything is one. God is not separate from the will of God. If the Kingdom of God is the will of God in force, then the Kingdom of God *is* God. More precisely the Kingdom of God is God insofar as God is redemptively present and active in the human heart, in the midst of a group of people, in a community, in institutions and movements, in the world at large, in nature, in the cosmos.

The Kingdom of God is a past, present, and future reality, since God is past, present, and future all at once. The Kingdom of God has already broken into history. We see reference after reference to it in the Old Testament. The

Kingdom of God is a present reality—our God is a living God, and the will of God is being fulfilled even now. Finally, the Kingdom of God is a coming, or future, reality. Indeed the Lord taught us to pray: "Thy Kingdom come, thy will be done . . ."

How does the Kingdom come about? First, it is always the Kingdom of *God*. God, not humans, brings about the Kingdom. On the other hand, God invites and requires human collaboration in the realization of the Kingdom. We are co-workers with God in the coming of God's final reign over all creation. Pope John Paul II forcefully makes this point in his 1981 encyclical letter, "On Human Work" (*Laborem exercens*), drawing from the creation accounts in Genesis.

Vatican II's Pastoral Constitution on the Church in the Modern World makes clear the terms of the relationship between divine and human effort in the coming of the Kingdom: "Earthly progress must be carefully distinguished from the growth of Christ's kingdom. Nevertheless, to the extent that the former can contribute to the better ordering of human society, it is of vital concern to the kingdom of God" (n. 39). Our human efforts don't create the Kingdom, but they are "of vital concern" to it. In other words, we don't know precisely how our efforts contribute to the coming of the Kingdom, but we do know that they have some significant connection with it. In the end, the council declares, our efforts on behalf of "human dignity, brotherhood and freedom, and indeed all the good fruits of our nature and enterprise" will be carried forward into the heavenly Kingdom, "but freed of stain, burnished and transfigured" (Pastoral Constitution on the Church in the Modern World, n. 39).

In summary, ministry is for the sake of the Church, and the Church is for the sake of the Kingdom of God. Ultimately all ministry, including general human ministry, is for the sake of the Kingdom of God. And the Kingdom, after all, is not something available only to Christians or to the Church. The Kingdom is for everyone. In fact, many people in the Kingdom are not in the Church, and many people in the Church are not in the Kingdom. "For in the ineffable foreknowledge of God," St. Augustine (d. 430) wrote in his treatise on baptism, "many who seem to be outside are within [and] many who seem to be within are outside."

In the final accounting "Not everyone who says to me, 'Lord, Lord,' will enter the kingdom of heaven, but only the one who does the will of my Father in heaven" (Matt. 7:21). Ministry helps God's will to be fulfilled for other people, for the Church, and for the whole world.

SUMMARY

1.   Although there are different approaches to ministry in recent theological writings and ecumenical documents, certain important points have been agreed upon: (1) ministry is rooted in the Holy Spirit; (2) there is a distinction between general and particular ministry; (3) all ministry is functional; that is, for the benefit of others, not primarily for the benefit of the minister; and (4) ultimately all ministry is for the sake of the Kingdom of God, which is the object of the Church's mission.

2.   Ministry functions at four levels:

- *General/universal ministry* is any service rendered to others, rooted in our humanity, and to be done by every human being.
- *General/specific ministry* is a special service rendered to others, rooted in competence, and to be done by those who are appropriately certified.
- *Christian/universal ministry* is any service rendered in Christ and because of Christ, rooted in baptism and confirmation, and to be done by every member of the Church.
- *Christian/specific ministry* is a Christian service rendered in the name of the Church and for the sake of its mission, rooted in some act of designation by the Church, and to be done by relatively few members of the Church.

3. Ministry is for the Church—the Body of Christ—and the Church is both an institution and a community, local and universal, denominational and ecumenical.

4. The mission of the Church is the proclamation, celebration, signification, and service of the Kingdom of God: *word, worship, witness,* and *service.*

5. The Kingdom of God *is* God, insofar as God is redemptively present and active in our hearts, in our communities, in our institutions and movements, in the world at large, in nature, in the whole cosmos. The Kingdom of God exists whenever and wherever the will of God is acknowledged and fulfilled.

6. Ultimately all ministry—Christian and non-Christian alike—is for the sake of the Kingdom of God.

DISCUSSION QUESTIONS

1. Do you think that one's particular tradition (Catholic, Lutheran, Presbyterian, Episcopalian, Greek Orthodox, and so on) makes much difference in the way one defines ministry? If so, how? If not, why not?

2. Do you think there has been too much or too little emphasis on ordained ministry? Do you regard recent theological and ecumenical developments as restoring some balance or making matters worse? Explain.

3. The definition of ministry is inextricably linked with the nature and mission of the Church. Do you think that differences of opinion about ministry, even within the same denomination, usually reflect more fundamental differences regarding the Church? Give examples.

4. What ministries do you think the Church could easily do without because they've outlived their purpose or usefulness? What types of ministries, not now on the books, will the Church have to develop as it moves into the next century?

5. If you were invited to speak at a seminary, what three points about ministry would you most want to make to students and faculty alike? What would you like to say to a class of permanent deacons on the night before ordination?

6. If you were the bishop of your diocese, what would you most like to do about the ministries of the diocese? If you were the pastor of your parish, what would you most like to

do about the parish's ministries?

7. If you were asked to put together an advertising campaign to interest more lay people in church ministries, how would you go about it? What points would you most emphasize?

SUGGESTED READINGS

Abbott, Walter M., and Joseph Gallagher, eds. *The Documents of Vatican II.* New York: Guild Press, America Press, Association Press, 1966. A basic reference. Most of the sixteen council documents are concerned with ministry of one kind or another.

Baptism, Eucharist and Ministry: Faith and Order Papers No. 111. Geneva: World Council of Churches, 1982. The so-called Lima document, which is the most important ecumenical statement on ministry.

Bavarel, Michel. *New Communities, New Ministries: The Church Resurgent in Africa, Asia, and Latin America.* Maryknoll, NY: Orbis Books, 1983. Ministries in the Third World.

Byers, David M., and Bernard Quinn. *New Directions for the Rural Church: Case Studies in Area Ministry.* New York: Paulist Press, 1978. Cooperative ministry in rural areas.

Bernardin, Joseph Cardinal. *In Service of One Another: Pastoral Letter on Ministry.* Chicago: Chicago Catholic Publishing Co., 1985. An example of how a theologically sophisticated and pastorally sensitive bishop approaches the topic.

Coll, Regina, ed. *Women and Religion: A Reader for the Clergy.* New York: Paulist Press, 1982. The place of women in ministry, addressed from different angles and experiences.

Empie, Paul C., and T. Austin Murphy. *Lutherans and Catholics in Dialogue IV: Eucharist and Ministry.* Washington, DC:

United States Catholic Conference, and New York: U.S.A. National Committee of the Lutheran World Federation, 1970. One of the most important ecumenical statements on ministry.

McBrien, Richard P. "Church and Ministry: the Achievement of Yves Congar." *Theology Digest* 32 (Fall 1985): 203–11.

O'Meara, Thomas F. *Theology of Ministry.* New York: Paulist Press, 1983. A contemporary Catholic approach.

Provost, James H., ed. *Official Ministry in a New Age.* Washington, DC: Canon Law Society of America, 1981. An important collection of papers on the theological, pastoral, and canonical aspects of ministry.

Schillebeeckx, Edward. *The Church with a Human Face: A New and Expanded Theology of Ministry.* New York: Crossroad, 1985. An important work by one of the Catholic Church's best-known theologians.

Schuller, David S., Merton P. Strommen, and Milo L. Brekke, eds. *Ministry in America: A Report and Analysis, Based on an In-Depth Survey of 47 Denominations in the United States and Canada, with Interpretation by 18 Experts.* San Francisco: Harper & Row, 1980.

Study on Priestly Life and Ministry: Summaries of the Report of the Ad Hoc Bishops' Subcommittees on History, Sociology and Psychology. Washington, DC: National Conference of Catholic Bishops, 1971.

Chapter 2

HOW HAS MINISTRY EVOLVED?

If it is difficult to define ministry, it is even more difficult to trace its history. There is no linear development from Jesus Christ to the apostles to the popes to the bishops all the way down to our own time. The only thing one can say for certain is that the present ministerial structure of the Catholic Church, or of any of the Christian churches, is not to be found as such in the New Testament itself.

This doesn't mean that none of its elements (for example, Petrine ministry, episcopacy, presbyterate, diaconate) is to be found in the Bible. Nor does it mean that certain postbiblical developments have necessarily contradicted the witness of the New Testament. It just means that the history of the Church's ministries isn't so clear-cut as some of us might have thought or have been led to believe.

Of course, Jesus didn't call his twelve apostles together one day and announce, "I've decided to establish a Church, a religion entirely separate from Judaism. I've also decided to give it a particular organizational structure. It will be an absolute monarchy, although it will appear at times like a modified oligarchy.

"Peter will be its first pope. What he says, goes. The other eleven of you will assist Peter in his work—which is to decide what's true and what's false, what's right and what's wrong, who shall enter heaven and who shall not. Obviously, he'll appreciate whatever help you can give him.

"Because of your missionary labors the Church is going to grow by leaps and bounds. When that happens, you're going to have to create more and more dioceses. Upon your death, you will be succeeded by others who will be called bishops, not apostles. They will be ordained by those of you who are still living and eventually by your successors. The function of a bishop is to be the primary teacher, ruler, and sanctifier of a diocese. That's the way it will be for all time. There will be an unbroken chain of bishops created by the laying on of hands and the recitation of a formula of ordination I will give you.

"Just as Peter needs you as his helpers, and just as you will need other bishops as your helpers and successors, so the bishops will need priests as their helpers. There will be thousands of dioceses, each administered by a bishop. And within each diocese there will be many more thousands of parishes, each administered by a pastor.

"Pastors will be assisted by other priests, known as curates or associates, and sometimes by deacons as well. Ordination is required in each instance. Lay persons, including even women, may also be asked to help out whenever the pastor thinks it suitable. At the parish level, everyone will be subject to the pastor. Pastors, in turn, will be subject to the bishops, and the bishops will be subject to the pope.

"You may wonder what happens after Peter dies. He

will have successors too. Otherwise the Church would be built on sand rather than on a rock. Peter's successors, however, won't be chosen in the same way *your* successors are to be chosen. The pope will be elected by cardinals. Normally a new pope will be chosen from within the College of Cardinals.

"The pope will have full and supreme power over the whole Church, including yourselves. He will appoint all bishops and all cardinals, but he will leave it up to the bishops to determine who should be ordained to the priesthood and the diaconate. The pope might decide to involve you in the governance of the Church. He can call ecumenical councils and synods of bishops. But he doesn't have to. The Church, if need be, can run very well under the pope alone. Is that clear?"

It may sound humorous to think of Jesus as a sort of CEO laying out a corporate structure for all time. Unfortunately many Catholics and other high-church Christians think that's about the way it happened, give or take the pope and a few cardinals. But it didn't happen that way. Ministry is not limited to the ministry of the ordained, nor has the ministerial structure of the Church been fixed for all time by the Lord's expressed will.

MINISTRIES IN THE NEW TESTAMENT

"In our study of first-century Christianity," British New Testament scholar James G. D. Dunn has written, "*we have discovered no greater diversity than that apparent in the various concepts of ministry.*" Professor Dunn's conclusion is based on findings contained in his *Unity and Diversity in the New Testament: An Inquiry into the Character of Earliest Christianity*, chapter 6, "Concepts of Ministry" (pp. 103–23). (See the suggested readings at the end of this chapter.)

According to Dunn and other biblical scholars, Catholic and Protestant alike, ministry even within the New Testament went through at least three stages:

1. pre-Easter discipleship, in which ministry was centered exclusively in Jesus himself;
2. first-generation Christianity, with two diverging patterns of ministry: (a) *charismatic*, as in the original Jerusalem community and later in Corinth, and (b) *structured*, based on the synagogue model;
3. second-generation Christianity, where the patterns became both intermingled, as in Acts, and more divergent, as in the Pastoral Epistles [1 and 2 Timothy and Titus] on the one hand, and the Johannine books [the Fourth Gospel and 1, 2, and 3 John], on the other.

If there is anything at all that one can confidently say about ministry in the New Testament, therefore, it is that there is a variety of ministries, a variety of combinations of ministries, and a variety of ministerial structures.

This is clear from the so-called classic passages concerning gifts, charisms, offices, and ministries of various kinds: 1 Corinthians 12:4–11; Romans 12:6–8; and Ephesians 4:11–16. There are ministries of preaching, instruction, healing, miracle-working, prophecy, the discernment of spirits, the interpretation of tongues, teaching, exhortation, almsgiving, presiding, works of mercy, and administration, as well as the ministry of the apostles, evangelists, and pastors. The most basic form of ministry in the New Testament was the ministry of the word in its various forms.

It should be said that the term *hiereus* (priest), which we find in Hebrews, applies only to Christ, who fulfilled the Old Testament notion of sacrifice and brought the Jewish cultic system to an end. Nowhere in the New Testament is *hiereus* used for someone who holds an office in the Church.

However, the term *hiereus* is applied to Christians in a few texts. The application in 1 Peter 2:9—"But you are a chosen race, a royal priesthood, a holy nation, a people of God's own"—is metaphorical and collective. It is a way of describing the elect and holy character of God's people, not the rights and privileges of individuals.

Redeemed Christians are also called priests in Revelation 1:6 ("[Jesus Christ] has made us into a kingdom, priests for his God and Father"); Revelation 5:10 ("priests for our God"); and Revelation 20:6 ("they will be priests of God and of Christ, and they will reign with him for [the] thousand years"). But the otherworldly character of this priesthood renders doubtful its significance for the present time. We simply don't know if the references in Revelation mean that each baptized person is a priest or if these texts are to be interpreted metaphorically, applying to the whole of God's people.

In any case the term *hiereus* could not have been used of Christian ministers until Christianity's separation from Judaism had become complete and definitive. Only in the last quarter of the second century A.D. did *hiereus* become a common designation for Christian officeholders. This occurred as recognition of the sacrificial nature of the Eucharist grew. The one who presided at the Eucharist was seen as exercising a priestly role.

What is clear is that the classic image of the Christian priest is really a fusion of several different roles: disciple, apostle, presbyter-bishop, and presider at the Eucharist. No serious biblical scholar and no serious theologian would argue today that the ministerial structure with which Catholics and other high-church Christians are familiar was already in place in the New Testament period, nor is there any evidence that such a structure was explicitly intended by Christ.

Before there was any formal community of faith, there was only discipleship, not ministry. The disciple was by definition a learner, someone who was on the way to perfection but with a long road yet to travel. The first formal ministry in the Church was that of the Twelve. Thereafter the original Jewish-Christian communities organized themselves according to the synagogue model with elders, prophets, and preachers.

But as the Church moved to culturally different communities through the ministry of the apostles, different models of ministry, with bishops and deacons, were adopted in and adapted to those places.

Ministry in the earliest years of the Church, therefore, was of two kinds: (1) ministry that flowed from the missionary enterprise and involved apostles, prophets, and teachers, and (2) ministry that consisted of the residential care of local communities—presbyters primarily (although not exclusively) in the Jewish-Christian communities, and bishops and deacons in the Gentile-Christian communities.

We find an integration of these two kinds of ministry in the Pastoral Epistles (Titus and 1 and 2 Timothy), but even there the precise relationship between bishops and deacons on the one hand and presbyters on the other is not clear. The New Testament yields no ecclesiastical blueprint in which the Church's many ministries are already securely in place, job descriptions and all. The watchwords instead are *pluralism, diversity,* and *variety.*

MINISTRIES IN THE POSTBIBLICAL CHURCH

Judging from the letters of St. Ignatius of Antioch (d. 108), the single bishop evidently was the pivotal figure in the local church. He had authority over the local presbytery (council of elders) and the deacons and jurisdiction over the administration of the sacraments. We see a development at work, therefore, but it is an uneven, almost erratic development and one dictated as much by politics as by theology or the inspiration of the Holy Spirit. As one reviews the history of the Church's ministries in the postbiblical period, one is struck by the parallels between the ministerial terminology and structures and the contemporary political terminology and structures. What follows is a brief summary of some of the more important aspects of that history.

The First Presbyters and Bishops

In the writings of Clement of Rome (d. ca. 96) presbyters are called leaders (*hegoumenoi*) of the community. Clement uses exactly the same term for civic officials in the city.

Clement contrasts presbyters, or elders, with "youngers," who resist the presbyters' leadership and guidance. Similar conflicts arose in civic administration. Alongside a leading council of elders (*gerousia*) there was an official council of "youngers" (*neoi*) who often had to defend different interests. Even the Greek word for church (*ekklesia*) is a political term, meaning "assembly," consisting of those eligible to conduct the affairs of the city.

In second-century Rome the political authority of the popular assembly and the city presbyters gave way to that of the governor. In decisions and elections the assembly had only the right of applause, or assent (about as meaningful as the applause that now rings out during ordination ceremonies), while the city presbyters exercised greater power. A similar development occurred in the Church's ministerial life.

The Letter of Polycarp to the Christian community of Philippi is addressed to the "presbyters and deacons," the leaders of the local church. There are no bishops. *Episcope*, "oversight" or "supervision," was performed by the presbyters. Neither is there any mention of bishops in the Didache, one of the most ancient and authoritative documents of the Church. We never find the singular word for supervisor (*episcopos*). Only the function (*episcope*) is mentioned, and that is applied to the whole body of presbyters. Alongside the presbyters are the older charismatic leaders, prophets and teachers.

How, then, did we arrive at Ignatius of Antioch's concept of the single bishop governing the single local church? Historians and theologians don't really know. Perhaps the ecclesiastical change paralleled a political change. In certain places in Asia Minor in the second half of the second century, councils of elders sometimes had two leaders, and sometimes they had only a single leader, or *archon*.

In richer cities an administrative supervisor (*episcopos*) functioned as the treasurer of the council, though not its leader. Because of his role he could attract a great amount of power and authority to himself. But how the distinction between presbyter (council member) and bishop (supervisor) came into being, we simply do not know. We only know that such a distinction did eventually develop, and that one of the presbyters became the head, or first *archon*, of the council of presbyters. Thus a new model of official ministry emerged. No community (*ekklesia*) assembled without the bishop. And, of course, there was no bishop without a community.

Other examples could be drawn from the experience of the Church in Rome, in Egypt, and in Africa during the second century. What is clear from all the evidence we have is that ecclesiastical developments followed a parallel course with political developments in the Roman empire. Shifts in civic administration produced shifts in ecclesiastical administration.

In some areas a hierarchy of bishops, metropolitans, and patriarchs came into being. Parallel to the diets of the empire, there developed regional synods of bishops and finally ecumenical councils of all bishops throughout the empire. By the end of the fourth century there were five great patriarchates: Jerusalem, Alexandria, Antioch, Constantinople, and Rome. Because Rome had been the seat of the empire, its bishop became the supreme leader of all bishops and patriarchs. He was later called "Pope" and exercised those functions in relation to the universal Church that had been ascribed to Peter in the New Testament.

The Institution of Ordination

Ministry became canonically and liturgically institutionalized by the first half of the third century. The *Traditio Apostolica* (Apostolic Tradition) of Hippolytus (d. 235), which influenced centuries of liturgical tradition, is the first major witness to the practice of ordination. The rites of ordination for bishops, presbyters, and deacons all had in common their reference to a particular community as the basis of authority.

Bishops.

First, a local community and its clergy selected its own bishop. The person selected was expected to obey the call, even against his own will. This happened in the cases of St. Ambrose (d. 397) and St. Augustine, for example. The community regarded the bishop's appointment as a gift of the Holy Spirit. For that reason he was installed by a laying on of hands and the *epiclesis*, or community's prayer to the Spirit. Because each local church regarded itself as part of a larger community of local churches, bishops from neighboring churches performed the function of the laying on of hands. According to the rite of ordination, the bishop's role is to proclaim God's word, forgive sins, preside over the Eucharist, and supervise the work of the presbyters and deacons.

Presbyters.

The ordination of a presbyter is performed by the laying

on of hands by the bishop and then by the presbyters of the local community. According to the rite of ordination, presbyters were compared with the elders whom Moses had chosen (Num. 11:17–25). They did not preside at the Eucharist but formed a ring, or crown, around the bishop as he presided. (This may be compared with our current rite of concelebration.) With the bishop's permission a presbyter could replace the bishop as the presiding eucharistic minister.

At this time there were no parishes, only dioceses, which covered entire towns. As the Church spread beyond the town limits presbyters assumed episcopal and sacerdotal responsibilities over these smaller rural communities. From that point on presbyters began to be known also as *sacerdotes* (priests). As a result the difference between bishops and the so-called country priests became blurred.

Deacons.

The ordination of a deacon was performed in the same way as that of a presbyter, except that the college of presbyters itself was not involved. The deacon at that time was tied exclusively to the service of the bishop. The deacon did not become a member of the college of presbyters, and his job description was entirely up to the bishop.

Prohibitions against Absolute Ordination.

Canon 6 of the Council of Chalcedon (451) condemned any form of "absolute consecration," that is, the ordination of anyone without reference to a particular community of faith. So strong is this canon that the ordination of anyone who was not called by a particular community was null and void. Anyone so ordained would not be paid by the state. (By the fifth century Christianity had become the official state religion.) His expenses would have to be borne by the bishop who had presumed to ordain him.

Later Isidore of Seville (d. 636) called those consecrated in an absolute way—that is, without a community to serve—headless people, "neither man nor beast." In any case it was a prohibition that was known and honored throughout the Church, both in the East and West, all the way down to the Council of Trent in the sixteenth century.

The Emerging Distinction between Clergy and Laity

In the early Church there was no hard-and-fast distinction between clergy and laity. All the baptized were members of Christ's Body. Some few of the baptized were "set apart" (the meaning of the word for clergy, *cleros*) for the service of the whole community. A division between clergy and laity began to develop with the establishment of Christianity as the state religion in the fourth century and with the transformation of the clergy into a kind of civil service, with all the political and economic privileges of rank and status.

The division between clergy and laity was widened during the Middle Ages when theologians and canonists divided the Church into two separate states: the *ordo clericorum* and the *ordo laicorum*. The latter was composed of men of the world, men given to the flesh. The former was composed of those devoted to the spiritual realm, responsible for the governance of the Church. The division was influenced also by a Neoplatonist view of the world, which defined reality as gradational and hierarchical, consisting of lower and higher forms. The clergy were at the higher end, with the pope at the very top, and the laity were at the bottom.

The Medieval Distinction between Power of Ordination and Power of Jurisdiction

Towards the end of the eleventh century another important distinction was made between the power of orders and the power of jurisdiction. Canon lawyers distinguished between the power of orders, which is the priestly power to celebrate the Eucharist and forgive sins, and the power of jurisdiction, which is the authority to exercise those priestly powers on behalf of a diocese, a parish, or a religious community.

This distinction separated priestly power, communicated in ordination, from *ministry*, or service to the People of God in a particular place. Thus if a man were ordained, even without the call of a community, he nevertheless received the power of orders to celebrate the Eucharist and to forgive sins. This would have been utterly unthinkable in the early Church and was actually prohibited by canon 6 of the Council of Chalcedon.

What would have explained so dramatic a change? Feudalism and legalism. Many bishops and priests were being ordained not for the service of any particular community but as status symbols of feudal lords, attached to the secular rulers' private churches. The bishops in turn came to adopt and imitate the political trappings of the secular princes and became themselves prince-bishops, with rings, croziers, and other insignia of office.

At the same time there was a renaissance of Roman law, which detached the power of leadership in every sphere from the concept of territoriality and therefore in the religious sphere detached leadership from the concept of local church. In other words, under the impact of the new legalism authority and power became values in themselves, independent of any basis in the community.

The ordained priesthood was seen increasingly as a "state of life" rather than as a ministry to a community of faithful Christians. On top of this privatization of the priesthood came the lawyers' concept of "sacred power," with its distinction between the power of ordination and the power of jurisdiction.

Thus although an ordained man might have had no call from a community (and therefore no need for or claim on the power of jurisdiction), by virtue of ordination he already possessed in his own person all the "priestly power" he would ever require to function as a priest. Such a priest could celebrate the Eucharist, even without a community (the so-called private Mass). Such a development would have been inconceivable in the early Church.

The Teachings of the Council of Trent

No event in the history of the Catholic Church between the Protestant Reformation of the sixteenth century and Vatican II (1962–65) shaped and influenced Catholic theology, catechesis, worship, spirituality, seminary education, and the like more profoundly than the Council of Trent.

The Council of Trent's approach to ministry, particularly the ordained ministry of the priesthood, was fashioned out of at least three different developments: (1) the interference of the lay nobility in the appointment of bishops and pastors, (2) the Reformers' critique of the ordained priesthood, and (3) feudalism's emphasis on a hierarchical system of authority and privilege. The Council of Trent reacted against the first two factors by emphasizing the ordained priesthood over against the priesthood of all the faithful but absorbed the third factor by reinforcing the pyramidal structure of pope, bishops, priests, deacons, and laity. In the absence of a balanced ecclesiology and a sound theology of ministry, the Council of Trent simply reinforced the conventional legalistic teachings of the day, including the distinction between the power of ordination and the power of jurisdiction.

This view of the priesthood was passed on within the Catholic Church without criticism or essential change all the way into the middle of the twentieth century. It is in evidence in the papal writings on the priesthood of Pius X, Pius XI, and Pius XII and remains the common understanding of many in the middle-to-senior generations of Catholics today. Priests are still regarded by many Catholics (including not a few priests) as having unique spiritual powers independently of any pastoral commitment to a particular congregation or community. Some priests, in fact, are still appointed as bishops for honorary or purely administrative purposes, as in the case of those who serve as heads of various Vatican agencies.

The permanent diaconate sometimes inadvertently provides examples of this unfortunate medieval distinction between the power of ordination and the power of jurisdiction, as well as of the pyramidal structure of the Church. A newly ordained permanent deacon is assigned to a parish that already has an adequate staff of well-trained lay ministers. Even though the deacon is not needed, he is inserted into the parish's ministerial network. And because he is ordained, he is accorded a status above all of his lay colleagues.

The Council of Trent's teaching on the ordained priesthood was reinforced in the seventeenth century by the so-called French school of priestly spirituality, which insisted that Christ's own priesthood is rooted in his divinity, not his humanity. Through ordination, therefore, priests share in a very mysterious, highly mystical power.

Such a view was also consistent with the ecclesiology of the post-Reformation Catholic Church. Everything was seen in the Church as coming "from above." "The Church" became simply the hierarchy. Bishops and priests were "churchmen" with special spiritual powers and authority rather than with a mandate to service. *Ministry* became identified more and more with Protestantism—as did the words *kingdom, fellowship,* and the like. Even in ordinary conversation we distinguish the pastoral leaders of the three major faiths that way—priests, *ministers,* rabbis.

The Teachings of Vatican II: Ministry as Service

The Second Vatican Council sought to reinstate the notion of ministry as service rather than ecclesiastical status. Ministry is no longer a word to be applied only to the ordained. There is "a variety of ministries" in the Church (Dogmatic Constitution on the Church, n. 18).

Moreover, the Church itself is no longer to be identified exclusively nor even primarily with the hierarchy. The

Church is the whole People of God (Dogmatic Constitution on the Church, chapter 2). All share, by baptism, in the threefold ministry of Jesus Christ as prophet, priest, and king. "Everything which has been said so far concerning the People of God applies equally to the laity, religious, and clergy." Indeed the lay apostolate is "a participation in the saving mission of the Church itself" (Dogmatic Constitution on the Church, nn. 30, 31).

Even though there are still some occasional references to the "sacred power" of the ordained priest, the medieval distinction between the power of orders and the power of jurisdiction is abandoned. Whatever power the minister has is always in the service of the People of God, of which the minister is also a member.

"By sacred ordination and by the mission they receive from their bishops," the council declared, "priests are promoted to the service of Christ, the Teacher, the Priest, and the King. They share in His ministry of unceasingly building up the Church on earth into the People of God, the Body of Christ, and the Temple of the Holy Spirit" (Decree on the Ministry and Life of Priests, n. 1).

But the Second Vatican Council's teaching is not without some ambiguity. For example, it insists that although all the faithful participate in the priesthood of Christ by baptism and confirmation (Decree on the Apostolate of the Laity, n. 3), there is nonetheless a difference not only "in degree" but "in essence" between "the common priesthood of the faithful and the ministerial or hierarchical priesthood" (Dogmatic Constitution on the Church, n. 10).

The faithful exercise their priesthood by joining in the

offering of the Eucharist, by receiving the sacraments, by offering prayer and thanksgiving, by giving witness through a holy life, and by practicing self-denial and active charity. The ordained priest, "by the sacred power he enjoys, molds and rules the priestly people" and acts "in the person of Christ" as he "brings about the Eucharistic Sacrifice, and offers it to God in the name of all the people" (Dogmatic Constitution on the Church, n. 10).

Neither did the council definitively clarify the relationship between bishops and presbyters. Bishops, the council declared, "enjoy the fullness of the sacrament of orders," whereas priests and deacons are "dependent upon them in the exercise of authority" (Decree on the Bishop's Pastoral Office in the Church, n. 15). Presbyters (priests) are "prudent fellow workers of the episcopal order," while deacons are "ordained for service and ministry to the People of God in communion with the bishop and his presbytery" (Decree on the Bishop's Pastoral Office in the Church, n. 15).

In the final accounting, however, Vatican II recovered the notion of ministry as service rather than as an ecclesiastical status. Whatever "sacred power" the ordained possess and exercise, it is always for the sake of the life and mission of the whole People of God, all of whom, by baptism and confirmation, participate in the one priesthood of Christ: "Pastors also know that they themselves were not meant by Christ to shoulder alone the entire mission of the Church toward the world. On the contrary, they understand that it is their noble duty so to shepherd the faithful and recognize their services and charismatic gifts that all according to their proper role may cooperate in this common undertaking with one heart" (Dogmatic Constitution on the Church, n. 30).

SUMMARY

1. The history of the Church's ministries and ministerial structures is complex and uneven. Ministry even within the New Testament period went through various stages, from pre-Easter discipleship to more highly structured forms of ministry in the Church's second generation.

2. In the first centuries following the New Testament period the Church's ministerial structures were strongly influenced by contemporary political developments. Thus councils of presbyters, or elders, were civic as well as ecclesiastical bodies. Their heads were supervisors (the meaning of the Greek word for "bishop").

3. Bishops were originally selected by the community but then installed by the laying on of hands by neighboring bishops in order to show that each community was part of a larger community of local churches.

4. Presbyters (priests) did not originally preside at the Eucharist. They presided only when the bishop could not be present or when the Church expanded beyond the territory of the towns and required more presiders.

5. Deacons were ordained for the service of the bishop, not for the community at large. The deacon's job description was determined by the bishop.

6. Absolute ordination, that is, ordination without the call

from a particular community, was forbidden by the Council of Chalcedon (451). This prohibition was set aside during the Middle Ages when the power of ordination was separated from the power of jurisdiction, that is, the authority the priest needed to exercise his ministry on behalf of a local church.

7. Clergy and laity were divided after Christianity became the official state religion and the ordained became part of the civil service.

8. The power of ordination (orders) and the power of jurisdiction became separated towards the end of the eleventh century because of the influence of feudalism and legalism. Priests were seen as having been ordained for the celebration of Mass rather than for the service of a community of faith.

9. The Council of Trent's teaching on ministry was fashioned in reaction against the interference of lay nobility in the appointment of bishops and priests and against Protestantism's critique of the ordained priesthood. Trent's teaching also reflected an ecclesiology, inspired in part by feudalism, that tended to exaggerate the hierarchical nature of the Church.

10. The Second Vatican Council corrected much of the trend toward separating service and spiritual authority by equating the Church with the whole People of God, by insisting that all the baptized participate somehow in the one priesthood of Christ and by emphasizing service rather than status in ordained ministry.

DISCUSSION QUESTIONS

1. Which aspects of the history of the Church's ministries do you think are least understood? What particular difficulties, if any, does this misunderstanding produce in the life of the Church today?

2. Given the close relationship between political and ecclesiastical developments in the early Church, how might the Church's ministries have developed if the Church had taken root in twentieth-century America rather than in the heart of the Roman empire?

3. Do you approve of the way bishops are selected today? If so, why? If not, how would you go about changing the system?

4. Does it surprise you that presbyters (priests) did not originally preside at the Eucharist? If the priest is not to be defined by his "sacred power" to "say Mass", how *would* you define his priesthood?

5. Do you favor the restoration of the permanent diaconate? What are the advantages and disadvantages of doing so?

6. In the earliest centuries of the Church's existence, priests were always ordained for the service of particular communities. What do you think of priests who are full-time biology teachers in high school, full-time diocesan financial officers, or full-time deans of law schools, and so on?

7. Trent and Vatican II offer two very different concepts of ordained ministry. To what extent are these two views still

competing with one another in the Church today? How do these two views reflect two different understandings of the nature of the Church itself?

SUGGESTED READINGS

Brown, Raymond E. *Priest and Bishop: Biblical Reflections.* New York: Paulist Press, 1970. A slightly dated but still valuable introduction to the New Testament data on ordained ministries.

———. *The Community of the Beloved Disciple.* New York: Paulist Press, 1979. This book challenges the conventional view that our familiar Catholic ministerial structures are found throughout the New Testament period.

———. *The Churches the Apostles Left Behind.* New York: Paulist Press, 1984. This book studies seven different churches of the New Testament period, uncovering among them a great diversity in ministerial life and structure.

Cooke, Bernard. *Ministry to Word and Sacraments: History and Theology.* Philadelphia: Fortress Press, 1976. A comprehensive study that might be too lengthy for beginners but is useful nonetheless as a reference book.

Dulles, Avery. *Models of the Church.* Garden City, NY: Doubleday, 1974. Chapter 10 shows how our ecclesiology affects our understanding of ministry.

Dunn, James G. D. *Unity and Diversity in the New Testament: An Inquiry into the Character of Earliest Christianity.* Philadelphia: Westminster Press, 1977. An important exegetical and historical study. Although the entire book is pertinent, chapter 6, "Concepts of Ministry," is particularly valuable.

Meeks, Wayne A. *The First Urban Christians: The Social World of the Apostle Paul.* New Haven: Yale University Press, 1983. Important for understanding the world in which the Church and its ministries were first formed.

Mitchell, Nathan. *Mission and Ministry: History and Theology in the Sacrament of Order.* Wilmington, DE: Michael Glazier, 1982. An excellent overview of the history and theology of the ordained priesthood from its roots in the Old Testament to the present day.

Schillebeeckx, Edward. *The Church with a Human Face.* (See the list of suggested readings for chapter 1.) Although the book provides many new historical insights into the development of the Church's ministries, the organization and style might not be entirely suitable for beginners.

Chapter 3

WHAT QUALITIES DO
MINISTERS NEED?

As I indicated in the introduction this book is meant for a broad cross-section of Christians—those now in ministry of whatever kind and at whatever level; those who might be contemplating ministerial service; those responsible for identifying and recruiting good candidates for ministry; those responsible for educating, training, and spiritually forming future ministers; those now engaged in some form of ministerial preparation; and those responsible for evaluating the pastoral performance of people already in ministry. Clearly all these people can, should, and do minister. What is offered in this chapter is a set of criteria by which persons in each of these categories can make informed and responsible judgments and decisions concerning their role in the Church's ministerial life.

It has to be said at the outset that some people resent and resist the application of standards to the Church's ministries, particularly to its ordained ministries of bishop and presbyter (priest). A vocation is supernatural, they insist.

You don't choose God; God chooses you. A retired Jesuit in Boston gave stark expression to this point of view in a letter to the archdiocesan weekly newspaper: "The priestly vocation is essentially a call from Our Lord to a supernatural commitment, a sacrament and a mystery of grace. In that context sociology has very little to offer."

Several years ago in the same archdiocese of Boston a pastoral letter on priestly formation took exactly the opposite position. Produced by a committee of New England Catholic bishops at the request of the New England regional conference, the letter conceded that a "vocation is from God, of course, but the Church must determine if the vocation is truly present in a particular case" (*A Letter on Priestly Formation*, October 1, 1979, p. 4).

The New England bishops also reaffirmed their belief in "the divine origin of a vocation." "At the same time," they insisted, "such a theology of vocations only increases our obligation to look at many human factors which are observable and which will give us strong hope that a vocation is present" (p. 12).

This judgment, the bishops correctly noted, is based on the traditional Scholastic principle that "grace builds on nature." In other words, no one can become a great preacher if he lacks the natural capacity to project his voice with clarity and force. And no one can become an effective counselor if she lacks the basic human virtues of patience and sensitivity.

"The call is from Christ," the committee of New England bishops acknowledged, "but He expects His Church to search the hearts and minds of men to determine if the vocation is true. This involves human judgment enlightened by divine grace" (pp. 12–13).

In support of this view the bishops could also have cited another traditional principle, this one taken from the First Vatican Council (1869–70): Our faith must be a reasoned faith, not a blind faith. Vatican I declared in its *Dei Filius* that "in order that the submission of our faith be conformed to reason, God willed that, joined to internal helps of the Holy Spirit, there be external proofs of His revelation." The assent of faith "is by no means a blind impulse of the mind" (*Documents of Vatican Council I: 1869–1870*, John F. Broderick, ed. Collegeville: The Liturgical Press, 1971, pp. 43, 44).

Therefore it is never legitimate to oppose, much less ridicule, the application of public standards and public criteria to candidates for ministry or to those already in ministry. To argue that a vocation is supernatural and that God chooses the future minister, not vice versa, begs a very important question, How do we know that God has chosen this particular person?

Is it enough that the individual himself or herself testify to this call? Are we really prepared to accept anyone for any ministry simply on the basis of the person's declaration that God is calling him or her to a particular ministry? No one can seriously defend such a view.

Then how *do* we decide whom to accept for training and whom to reject? We must have some criteria that we expect candidates to meet. And this raises the question, What are those criteria?

Whatever criteria the Church employs must be consistent with the history and theology of ministry, as outlined in the first two chapters. It is a matter of basic logic that you have to know *what* you need before you can decide *who* can help meet that need. You have to know what ministry is and what particular ministries are for before you can determine which kinds of candidates might be best suited for ministry in general and for a particular ministry. You have to have some sense of a ministry's job description before you can begin matching candidates with ministries. These principles apply to people already in ministry just as surely as they apply to candidates for ministry. They are guidelines not only for the processes of recruiting and formation but also for the process of ongoing evaluation.

The first four criteria taken together—human wholeness, the theological virtues, the moral virtues, and a positive sense of the Church—constitute what is meant by Christian holiness. Every minister has to be an example of it, but the more public the ministry and the greater its responsibility for the life and mission of the Church, the greater the call to Christian holiness. The last three criteria—communication skills, theological competence, and social awareness—indicate the human qualities needed over and above those associated directly with Christian holiness.

BASIC HUMAN WHOLENESS

No matter which ministry is at issue every candidate and every minister must exhibit basic human wholeness. In other words, each must be a *healthy* person in mind and in body. Again, the pertinent principle is "grace builds on nature."

You cannot give what you don't have. You can't become a catechist or religious educator if you can't even provide a stranger with uncomplicated directions from one city block to the next. Catechesis and religious education are teaching ministries. They require teaching skills, which include the ability to explain things in a clear, orderly, and interesting manner.

Nor can you become a preacher or enter a ministry that requires public speaking if you freeze in the presence of a crowd or if you have an uncontrollable stutter. Nor can people with deep-seated emotional problems expect the Church to welcome them with open arms into ministries that require psychic serenity and self-confidence. Mentally unhealthy people almost inevitably project their own problems onto others. If a minister is pathologically guilt-ridden, that minister won't be satisfied until his or her pastoral "client" feels just as guilty about some form of human behavior as the minister feels.

Just about every person reading this book can probably think of at least one instance where an unstable parish or diocesan minister created unnecessary problems for people committed to their pastoral care.

Grace builds on nature.

THE THEOLOGICAL VIRTUES

Is it really too much to expect that those who present themselves for the service of the Church should be people of virtue? A virtue is, literally, a "power" (from the Latin word, *virtus*). It is a power to realize some moral good and to do it joyfully and with perseverance in spite of obstacles.

The *theological virtues* are those that have been infused by God: faith, hope, and charity.

Faith

Faith involves conviction, trust, and commitment. The object of faith is God. Indeed God is the *only* object of faith. To be a person of faith, therefore, is to be someone who is convinced (and lives by the conviction) that there is more to life than meets the eye, that there is a spiritual dimension beyond the material world, and that all reality comes from the creative hand of God and is sustained and guided by God's providential power and care.

It goes without saying that every one of the Church's ministers must be people of faith. They must believe in a living God who is present and active in our lives, in history, and in the world at large. But in the spirit of the First Vatican Council, faith is not credulity. Blind faith is no faith. Our faith must always be consistent with reason. It doesn't mean that we can argue our way into faith. It's still a gift, a virtue infused by God.

There are people who claim to have (or are thought by others to have) a deep faith, but they are really projecting their own psychological problems onto the world around them. How can one tell the difference between a person of authentic faith and a person of inauthentic faith, or credulity? If those who recruit, educate, and evaluate ministers are themselves healthy people, they will know the difference. People of authentic faith are able to recognize authentic faith in others by something that St. Thomas Aquinas called "a knowledge of connaturality." Just as priests and nuns in civilian clothes have a nose for other priests and nuns in civilian clothes, so do people of faith have a practical instinct that helps them sort out the authentic from the inauthentic. Which is not to say that it is all a matter of pastoral instinct. Of course there are other objective criteria—the candidate's expressed understanding of the major elements of the faith (God, Christ, salvation, the nature and mission of the Church, etc.), as well as the candidate's public living out of that faith. A candidate who claims to believe in Jesus Christ should show some signs of being a forgiving, compassionate, and generous person.

No test, however, is more important than the existence or absence of a sense of humor. People who claim to have deep faith but who look as if they'd break in two if they laughed are people who don't see reality in its proper perspective.

In theological terms those with an inauthentic faith have confused something less than God with God. It might be their strict and demanding human father, a particularly severe teacher, a religiously fanatical spouse, or some other strange person who embodies for them qualities that they attribute to God.

Sometimes they attribute divine qualities to authority figures in the Church, especially the pope. When they hear the pope criticized, it sounds blasphemous to them. The pope for them is a mythical person who embodies the presence and authority of God. When the pope speaks, God speaks—no matter what the topic, no matter what the occasion, no matter what the format. (Of course, few people are fully consistent. Oftentimes people of this mentality conveniently ignore the pope's teaching on social justice, human rights, and peace.)

Hope

Hope enables us to take responsibility for the future, both our personal future and that of the world in which we live. Hope, therefore, is always oriented toward the Kingdom of God. Hope measures everything against the future Kingdom of God, and so it is a virtue with an especially prophetic edge to it.

Like all virtues, hope stands in the middle between *presumption* and *despair*. Presumption sins against hope by excess; we presume that God will save us, regardless of what we do or what effort we make. Despair sins against hope by defect; we despair of ever achieving salvation, no matter what we do, or even what God does. Hope is as much a cardinal virtue as faith and charity. The absence of hope is as serious a deficiency in a minister or in a candidate for ministry as the absence of faith or love. Too often we seem to forget that.

Why else do we allow ourselves to confuse pessimism with a truly spiritual attitude? There are many people in today's Church who speak and act as if the world is going to hell on the fast track. Sometimes they say the same thing about the Church itself. Pessimism is no virtue. Looking upon the world and its human history as nothing more than "a vale of tears" denies the dignity and redemptive possibilities of God's own creation (see Rom. 8:18–25).

The Church's ministers must be hopeful people, which is not to say that they must be naively optimistic. Optimism is no virtue either. Hope is different from mere optimism. Hope is grounded in faith—in a faith that sees creation and history as guided and protected always by the creative and healing hand of God and in a faith in the promises of God that in the end the Kingdom will be given in all its fullness.

Charity

Charity enables us to participate in the life of God who *is* love (1 John 4:8, 16). Charity is lived faith and lived hope. It is love of God and love of neighbor, that is, the total dedication and devotion to the welfare of the other, regardless of the sacrifices required and regardless of the personal cost. Such love is rooted in the Cross and empowered by the Resurrection.

Love is possible, however, only for personally mature people, namely, those who can accept themselves and others for who and what they are. Jesus reminded us that we cannot really love our neighbor unless we first can love ourselves. Those who reject themselves tend to reject others as well.

The opposite of love is not hate; it's apathy, which is a suspension of commitment, a lack of concern. Love is the soul of all the other Christian virtues. Without it, St. Paul insisted, we are nothing more than "a resounding gong or a clashing cymbal" (see 1 Cor. 13:1–13). It should also go without saying, therefore, that every minister of the Church, regardless of the ministry he or she exercises or aspires to exercise, must be a loving person, ready at all times to sacrifice his or her individual interests to the needs of others.

People who aren't mature aren't capable of real love. They relate to people on the basis of their *own* needs, not the needs of the other. For them every human relationship is potentially exploitative and manipulative. We call this psychological condition narcissism. The narcissist has no place in ministry—which is not to say that the narcissist has no place in the Church. But it is the task of qualified ministers to help the narcissist transcend his or her self-centeredness and reach out to others in an authentically loving way.

Because charity is so central and indispensable to the Christian life, it is central and indispensable to Christian ministry. And because charity depends so much on a healthy personality ("grace builds on nature" again), we need the resources of modern science to help us determine who is sufficiently healthy to exercise certain ministries. Psychological testing of candidates, therefore, is essential for the most important ministries of pastoral leadership, particularly the presbyterate.

Candidates who manifest relatively minor personality disorders can be brought to new levels of personal maturity. Candidates who manifest more deeply rooted disorders have to be rejected, for their own sakes as well as the Church's.

If the Church admits such people to candidacy, the Church runs the serious risk of alienating the healthy candidates with whom an unhealthy candidate will be expected to live, work, and pray. Unhealthy ministers also lower the public image of a particular ministry and thereby discourage qualified candidates from even considering a vocation to that ministry.

"So faith, hope, love remain, these three; but the greatest of these is love" (1 Cor. 13:13).

THE MORAL (CARDINAL) VIRTUES

The *moral,* or *cardinal, virtues* are those that have to be acquired through cooperation with God's grace and that in turn are the linchpins of other, lesser virtues. The moral virtues are prudence, justice, temperance, and fortitude.

Prudence

Prudence is the ability to discern, to make moral choices. It answers the question, What is the best way for me, in this situation, to do the right thing? It involves conducting an inquiry, taking counsel from others, judging, and then making a decision. St. Thomas Aquinas called prudence the "rudder virtue." Without prudence a person is like a ship drifting aimlessly at sea.

Prudent people profit from their experience, have an instinct for asking the right people the right questions, have the foresight to anticipate difficulties and to see the consequences of their moral decisions, and, finally, can sift through all that they have learned and then make a decision consistent with the situation and circumstances before them.

If ministerial candidates are known by a significant number of respected parishioners, their prudence will not be hard to determine. Their reputations will have preceded them. A minister without prudence is a danger to the Church. Good judgment is not a luxury in ministry; it is an absolute necessity.

Justice

Justice is concerned with rights and with the duties that correspond to those rights. A right is a power to do whatever is necessary for achieving the end or purpose for which we are destined as human beings.

Since we are radically social beings, justice is concerned with our social relationships at various levels. The minister and ministerial candidate must be just at every level. *Commutative justice* gives each person his or her due; *distributive justice* gives all persons in a social grouping what is due them from the community's resources; *legal justice* gives the government and other responsible agencies what is due them for the sake of the common good; and *social justice* contributes out of one's resources and gifts to the common good of the society at large.

A minister or ministerial candidate who is unjust in his or her dealings with others is obviously not a fit person for ministry. But neither is one who is indifferent to issues of justice or who simply doesn't get involved when others are victimized by unfair practices and procedures, whether inside or outside the Church.

As a basic minimum all ministers and all candidates for ministry must be aware of and faithful to the Church's social teachings, as contained in various papal encyclicals from Pope Leo XIII to the present pope, in the Second Vatican Council's Pastoral Constitution on the Church in the Mod-

ern World (*Gaudium et spes*), in various synodal documents
(for example, *Justice in the World*, by the Third International
Synod of Bishops [1971]), and in various pastoral letters and
pronouncements of national episcopal conferences (for example, the United States Catholic bishops' letters on peace
and the economy).

Church members whose own political, social, and economic interests prevent them from readily accepting the
substance of Catholic social teachings ought to be discour-
aged from entering ministry, particularly ministries of pastoral leadership.

Temperance

Temperance enables us to achieve some balance in the
exercise of what the textbooks call our concupiscible appetites: our desires for food, drink, sex, tobacco, and other crea-
ture comforts. Temperance humanizes but does not repress
those human pleasures. (The only "pleasure" morally evil in
itself is the use of tobacco, given all that is now known about
its physically harmful effects on users and innocent by-
standers alike.)

The cardinal virtue of temperance is closely allied with
Christian asceticism, which is concerned, literally, with
those "exercises" that help us regulate the conflict between
the spirit and the flesh. It involves painful struggle, self-denial, and renunciation. Patterned on the Cross, asceticism is
obedience to the will of God even to the point of death, and
it leads to the service of others.

Church members who eat too much, drink too much, or
are consumed with lust should not be encouraged to pursue

what they believe to be a ministerial vocation, at least not until they have tried to bring their unruly appetites under some measure of control. Those who smoke should be encouraged to give up the habit. Young people who have initiated the smoking habit, despite all that is known today about its harmful effects, should be held to a particularly rigorous standard.

Fortitude

Fortitude enables us to overcome an instinctive fear in order to pursue the good. It brings balance to what the textbooks call our irascible appetites—fear and rashness. Fortitude has an active and a passive side—taking bold action for the sake of the Kingdom of God (see chapter 1) and enduring pain, suffering, and even death for the sake of the Kingdom.

People absolutely committed to never rocking the boat are without fortitude. People who do not have the courage of their convictions, who will not speak up or speak out in "prudence" for what is right and against what is wrong and unjust, lack the cardinal virtue of fortitude.

In conclusion it must be said that all of these virtues, theological and moral alike, are closely interrelated. You cannot have one without the others. Thus those who are prudent can never use their prudence as an excuse not to act with courage (fortitude). Those with fortitude cannot act without charity. Indeed Christians, and Christian ministers in particular, are always called to a life of *mercy*. Mercy, unlike justice, gives to others *more* than they deserve or have a right to.

Ministers and ministerial candidates must be Christians who practice both the *corporal works of mercy*—feeding the hungry, giving drink to the thirsty, clothing the naked, sheltering the homeless, visiting the sick, ransoming the captive, and burying the dead—and the *spiritual works of mercy*—instructing the ignorant, counseling the doubtful, admonishing the sinner, bearing wrongs patiently, forgiving offenses, comforting the afflicted, and praying for the living and the dead. Mercy reminds us that our obligations to others go beyond even the demands of social justice. It goes without saying that a merciless minister is a contradiction in terms.

A POSITIVE SENSE OF THE CHURCH

Ministers and candidates for ministry at whatever level cannot be fundamentally in doubt about the necessity and purpose of the Church. All ministry is in the service of the Church. It has no other purpose than to serve the People of God and to advance the mission they have received from Christ. Ministers and ministerial candidates must also have a practical understanding of and commitment to the gospel consistent with ecclesial faith, or faith in the Church.

This is not to say that ministers and ministerial candidates cannot be critical of the Church, whether as a family of people or as an hierarchical institution. The Church is a mystery, or sacrament, to be sure, but it is also a human community, with human structures and a rather uneven historical record besides. Vatican II itself acknowledged that the Church is "at the same time holy and always in need of being purified, and incessantly pursues the path of penance and renewal" (Dogmatic Constitution on the Church, n. 8).

The British philosopher John Stuart Mill said that our love for an institution is in proportion to our desire to reform it. Those who see no institutional problems at all in the Church may be too naive for ministerial service—or they may be in for a rude awakening when they take up their ministerial posts. Those who resent criticisms of the Church may lack an adequate ecclesiology for effective ministry. The Church is no ordinary community, to be sure. It is the Body of Christ and the Temple of the Holy Spirit. But it is not yet the Kingdom of God. At most the Second Vatican Council calls it the "initial budding forth" of the Kingdom (Dogmatic Constitution on the Church, n. 5).

The inevitable gap between the Kingdom promised and the Kingdom realized to date provides the space within which Church members can lovingly challenge the Church in order that it might be more faithful to its call and to its mission. But the key word here is *lovingly*. Criticism of the Church that is rooted in a persistent and corrosive anger or that expresses one's own sickness and cynicism is not consistent with that love of the Church at the heart of every ministry. Psychological testing, the judgment of prudent people, or both can usually sort out healthy criticism from unhealthy criticism.

COMMUNICATION SKILLS

Beyond the preceding criteria ministry in most instances requires the ability to facilitate communication and to be open to and profit from feedback. Insofar as ministry is always in the service of community (the Church) and community is always created and sustained by communication (ultimately, by the self-communication of the Holy Spirit), every minister and ministerial candidate must exhibit at least a basic aptitude for communication. The ability to communicate is especially necessary in such ministerial tasks as preaching, teaching, counseling, group leadership, and pastoring.

How often do we read in the newspaper or hear on television news of individuals who have gone berserk, shooting up convenience stores, post offices, college campuses, quiet residential neighborhoods, even churches? Inevitably people are asked if they knew the person. What was he like? Was there anything in his everyday behavior that might have given a warning? Almost always people characterize the person as a "loner." The man "always kept to himself." He "didn't bother anybody." He "didn't seem to have any friends," and he certainly had no women friends.

The Church doesn't have to fear an influx of potential mass murderers, but it *does* have to be on constant guard against the influx of loner types, people uncomfortable with themselves, uncomfortable with others, unable to communicate. In the past we sometimes confused incommunicativeness with sanctity. Just the opposite is true. Holiness is wholeness. The word *salvation*, after all, means "health" in Latin (*salus*). To be cut off from one's neighbors is to be cut off from God, for love of neighbor and love of God are two sides of the same coin of virtue. Only healthy people can communicate with others. The Church needs healthy ministers.

SOUND THEOLOGICAL COMPETENCE
AND VISION

The Christian minister must have a basically correct sense of the Church, not just a "positive" sense of the Church but a theologically sound sense as well.

The minister must know who Jesus Christ really is, not as a plaster statue but as the New Testament and Christian history and doctrine present him. He is fully human and fully divine. To deny his humanity is just as serious a doctrinal error as to deny his divinity. The Church has rejected both Monophysitism (which held that the humanity of Jesus was somehow absorbed by his divinity) and Nestorianism (which held that Jesus was a fully human person as well as a divine person). By the mystery of the Incarnation, Jesus is one divine person with both a human and a divine nature. The minister must also know what the Redemption is all about and how it relates to our identity as human beings. We have not been redeemed *from* our humanity. We have been redeemed from all those evil forces which undermine and indeed rob us of our God-given humanity. To sin, after all, is to act against who we are by birth and who we have become by baptism into the risen Christ.

Negatively the minister cannot embrace theological views so idiosyncratic (and that's the key word here) that they are clearly extreme even by the most progressive or the most conservative of theological standards. In other words, the Church has to beware of ministers and ministerial candidates whose left-wing views on important theological issues would shock even Hans Küng or whose right-wing views would distress even Cardinal Joseph Ratzinger. Accordingly, it would be wrong, on the one hand, to portray Jesus as if he were no more than a great social reformer, a liberationist par excellence. And it would be wrong, on the other hand, to view the pope as if he were a quasi-divine figure whose policies and opinions are directly inspired by God.

We do not look for theological sophistication of a very high order in all of the Church's ministers. The level of sophistication must be proportionate to the level of the ministry to which the candidate aspires. On the other hand, the Church has a right to exclude from any ministry a candidate whose theological views are clearly peculiar or extreme.

The more theological, historical, and biblical education a future minister can be exposed to, the better. Too many people in ministry or aspiring to ministry are theologically naive, historically ignorant, and biblically fundamentalistic. The Church is never well served by bad theology, bad history, and bad biblical interpretation. But this is not a matter simply of personal preference. Theology has to be consistent with the facts of history, with ecclesiastical teachings, and with developments in related disciplines such as sociology, psychology, and biblical exegesis. The interpretation of the Bible in its turn has to be guided by rules and principles that have been accepted by recognized scholars and approved by the Church. One finds these norms, for example, in Pope Pius XII's encyclical *Divino Afflante Spiritu* (1943), in the Pontifical Biblical Commission's *Instruction on the Historical Truth of the Gospels* (1964), and in the Second Vatican Council's Dogmatic Constitution on Divine Revelation (1965).

SOCIAL, POLITICAL, AND CULTURAL AWARENESS

Correlative with theological vision is social, political, and cultural awareness. Among other things this requires, especially in some of the more important pastoral leadership ministries, a comprehensive understanding of and commitment to Catholic social teachings, as well as some evidence of a practical and effective engagement in the Church's social apostolate.

In the early Church of Rome, for example, deacons were the leaders of the social apostolate and their presence at the altar served as a reminder to the assembled congregation of its own abiding call to the service of those in need. It would be anomalous, therefore, if the Church were to ordain as deacons men or (eventually) women who displayed no prior interest in or commitment to Catholic social teachings as they apply to human rights, social justice, and peace. The same would be true of other important ministries.

Those who sometimes pride themselves on never watching television or never following news events actually convict themselves of a lack of readiness for important ministries in the Church. To be indifferent to the social, economic, political, and cultural contexts of the people they are called to serve is, in effect, to deny the incarnational principle, whereby "the Word became flesh and made his dwelling among us" (John 1:14).

To be indifferent to the people, the places, the events, and the things in which the Word has become flesh is tantamount to being indifferent to the Word itself. Indeed it is impossible to grasp the Word or to be grasped by it apart from the human and natural condition in which it inserts itself continually. The minister and ministerial candidate, therefore, must be ever prepared to read the "signs of the times" and then to interpret them "in the light of the gospel" (Pastoral Constitution on the Church in the Modern World, n. 4).

Since every ministry of whatever kind and at whatever level is for the sake of the Church's life and mission, the Church's regard for the quality of ministry and for the qualifications of ministers will be as high or as low as its regard for the nature and mission of the Church itself. To settle for less in ministry—*any* ministry—is to settle for less in the quality of the Church's life and in the fulfillment of the Church's mission. Christians are disciples, after all, of the One who calls each to perfection (Matt. 5:48).

Christians are convinced in faith that what they do as ministers is rooted in what Jesus Christ did and continues to do as God's Suffering Servant, who came not to be served but to serve (Matt. 10:45). To be a minister, therefore, is to be a minister not for oneself or by oneself but for the Church and with the Church. The Church's ministries are collaborative in every sense of the word. "There are different kinds of spiritual gifts but the same Spirit; there are different forms of service but the same Lord; there are different workings but the same God who produces all of them in everyone" (1 Cor. 12:4).

SUMMARY

1. Criteria are necessary in the recruitment, formation, selection, and evaluation of ministers because grace builds on nature and our faith must always be a reasoned faith, supported to some extent by visible signs.

2. There are at least seven fundamental criteria the Church must employ in its recruitment, training, selection, certification, and evaluation of its ministers: (1) basic human wholeness, (2) theological virtues, (3) moral (cardinal) virtues, (4) a positive sense of the Church, (5) communication skills, (6) sound theological competence and vision, and (7) social, political, and cultural awareness.

3. Basic human wholeness refers to a quality of mental and physical health, necessary to fulfill a given ministry.

4. The theological virtues are faith, hope, and charity, and the moral (cardinal) virtues are prudence, justice, temperance, and fortitude.

5. Authentic faith is never fanatical or naive. A sense of humor may be the most reliable indicator of the presence of a strong and mature faith.

6. The Church's ministers must always be hopeful people, because of their faith in God's promise of the future Kingdom. A brooding, angry pessimism is incompatible with the call to Christian ministry.

7. Charity, or Christian love, presupposes a healthy personality. Love is at the core of every ministry. Narcissistic, or self-centered, people are not mature enough to minister effectively.

8. Prudence, the "rudder virtue," is the capacity for sound judgment. Imprudent ministers pose an ever-present threat to the credibility and effectiveness of the Church's ministerial life.

9. Justice is of various kinds, but it is essentially concerned with the rights of others. Ministers must be not only just men and women but also people committed to the Church's teachings on social justice, human rights, and peace.

10. Temperance is concerned with the control of our concupiscible appetites—inordinate desire for food, drink, and sex. The Christian minister must be a person of asceticism, prepared always to renounce whatever stands in the way of effective service of others.

11. Fortitude is Christian courage. It is concerned with the control of our irascible appetites (fear and rashness) and with taking action or enduring pain for the sake of the Kingdom of God.

12. Mercy tempers justice. Unlike justice, mercy gives to others more than they have a right to. The Christian minister must practice both the corporal and the spiritual works of mercy.

13. A positive sense of the Church does not exclude loving criticism of the Church.

14. Because ministry is always in service of a community of faith, every minister must have the capacity to communi-

cate. Community is impossible without communication.

15. A minister must have a sound theological perspective but must not be theologically idiosyncratic or extreme.

16. Because of the incarnational principle ("the Word became flesh and dwelt among us"), ministers must be aware of and concerned about the persons, events, places, and things in which the Word has inserted itself and continues to dwell.

17. Our seriousness about standards for ministry is an indication of our seriousness about the nature and mission of the Church itself.

DISCUSSION QUESTIONS

1. Can you think of other important criteria for ministry that you would like to see added to this chapter? Would you subtract one or more of the criteria offered here?

2. What criteria for ministry seem to be operative in your parish, diocese, or religious community? Are they consistent with the theology and history of ministry, as presented in the first two chapters?

3. To what extent does personality play a part in the difficulties you have experienced in pastoral ministry? Do you think we should pay more or less attention to psychological testing and counseling for ministry? Why?

4. Of the three theological virtues, which do you think is in the shortest supply among today's ministers? Explain.

5. Why does the quality and effectiveness of our individ-

ual ministries depend so much on the institutional context in which we try to exercise those ministries? Give examples.

6. How does the Church most obviously fail to live up to its own standards in the way it deals with its ministers? How do the Church's ministers most often fail to fulfill their ministerial responsibilities? Can anything be done about either problem?

7. Do you think temperance is a problem for many in ministry today? Explain. What about fortitude?

8. Do you think that someone who never criticizes the institutional Church, at least in public or where two or three are gathered together, can really be an effective minister? Conversely, can criticism ever get to the point where it harms one's ministry?

9. What books of theology, biblical studies, or church history have you read in the past six months? From where do you derive most of your information about developments in theology, in sacred Scripture, and in the life of the Church? Does such information really make any difference in your ministry and in the ministry of others?

10. Do you detect any correlation between a minister's lack of interest in current events and the minister's all-around effectiveness as a minister?

SUGGESTED READINGS

Bernardin, Joseph Cardinal. *In Service of One Another: Pastoral Letter on Ministry.* Chicago: The Chicago Catholic Publishing Co., 1985. A practical reflection on the nature and demands of ministry in today's Church by one of the United States Catholic Church's most pastorally effective bishops.

Hoge, Dean R. *The Future of Catholic Leadership: Responses to the Priest Shortage*. Kansas City, MO: Sheed & Ward, 1987. The most important single study, based on years of research and surveys, of the current crisis in presbyteral vocations. Must reading for bishops, seminary faculty and staff, vocation directors, and everyone else who has ever expressed an opinion about the subject.

Hoge, Dean R., Raymond H. Potvin, and Kathleen M. Ferry. *Research on Men's Vocations to the Priesthood and the Religious Life*. Washington, DC: United States Catholic Conference, 1984. Contains much useful information that serves as a corrective to more "pious" analyses of the problem.

Kwatera, Michael. *The Liturgical Ministry of Deacons*. Collegeville, MN: The Liturgical Press, 1985. Explains the duties of the deacon within the liturgy. For both permanent and transitional deacons.

McBrien, Richard P. *Catholicism*. San Francisco: Harper & Row, 1981. For those who want a comprehensive, encyclopedic statement of Catholic doctrine and theology, I humbly recommend this one-volume study edition.

Sullivan, Bishop Walter. "What Priesthood Awaits the Seminarian?" *Origins* 11/14 (September 17, 1981): 209, 211–13. A bishop tells it like it is.

Chapter 4

WHAT IS MINISTERIAL
SPIRITUALITY?

It is never enough simply to be a competent, efficient minister. The minister must embody and live by the spiritual values that she or he represents, proclaims, and tries to persuade others to embrace.

In keeping with the principle of sacramentality the minister is not only an instrument of God's grace; the minister is also a *sign* of God's grace. The invisible reality of grace must be made visible in the sign. And the sign in turn must truly embody the invisible reality it signifies. The sign signifies what it bears within itself.

To be in touch with the sign, therefore, is to be in touch with the reality it signifies. Otherwise it is a false sign, disconnected from the reality of grace it is supposed to signify. For this reason this century's greatest Catholic theologian, Father Karl Rahner, S.J., insisted that "it is not a matter of indifference to the meaning and nature of ministry in the Church whether it is exercised and administered with holiness or not" (*The Church and the Sacraments* [New York:

Herder, 1963], p. 98). In fact, there would be no holy Church if all of its members, ministers and nonministers alike, were sinners. Why? Because the Church is people, the People of God. The "holiness of the Church is only present and existent in the holiness of individuals, the multitude in fact who actually form the Church which is holy" (*The Church and the Sacraments*, p. 105). Moreover, there would be no sacraments and no ministerial life at all if the Church's ministers were "unbelieving and void of divine love." For it is "believing love" that "induces even the faithless and the loveless in the Church to deeds which essentially really spring from faith and love" (*The Church and the Sacraments*, p. 102).

Every ministry calls for a response of faith and love. But faith and love can only be called forth by "believing love" and loving faith. The minister, therefore, does more than provide a "service." The minister *witnesses* to the reality he or she communicates. In Rahner's view, "it is only really possible to bear witness to the faith by being a Christian oneself, that is, by one's own 'holiness' " (*The Church and the Sacraments*, p. 105).

This final chapter is concerned with the unity of sign and spiritual reality in those who minister in and for the Church. It is concerned, that is, with integrity, wholeness, and holiness.

SPIRITUALITY

"For those who live according to the flesh are concerned with the things of the flesh, but those who live according to the spirit with the things of the spirit" (Rom. 8:5). To be spiritual means to know and to live according to the knowledge that there is more to life than meets the eye. To be spiritual means, beyond that, to know and to live according to the knowledge that God is present to us in grace as the principle of personal, interpersonal, social, and even cosmic transformation. To be open to the Spirit is to accept explicitly who we are and who we are called always to become and to direct our lives accordingly.

The term *spirituality*, therefore, embraces everything that we are, think, and do in relation to the triune God who is present in and yet transcends all that is. Spirituality might be defined as *a style of life that flows from the presence of the Spirit within us and within the Church, the Temple of the Holy Spirit.*

The Second Vatican Council laid to rest, once and for all, the assumption that spirituality is for priests and nuns alone. The fifth chapter of its keynote Dogmatic Constitution on the Church is entitled, "The Call of the Whole Church to Holiness." The Lord himself was addressing *all* his disciples, regardless of their status or situation, when he said, "So be perfect, just as your heavenly Father is perfect" (Matt. 5:48).

We are, of course, already holy by reason of the Spirit's indwelling within us, and that indwelling is in turn rooted in the creative act of the Father and the redemptive work of the Son. Christian spirituality is a matter of living in accordance with who we have become in the Spirit, of manifesting the fruits of the Spirit's presence: mercy, kindness, humility, meekness, patience, and the like (Col. 3:12; Gal. 5:22; Rom. 6:22).

"Thus it is evident to everyone," the council declared, "that all the faithful of Christ of whatever rank or status are called to the fullness of the Christian life and to the perfection of charity." Significantly the council amplified on this declaration: "By this holiness a more human way of life is promoted even in this earthly society" (Dogmatic Constitution on the Church, n. 40). Holiness, therefore, is not only for everyone. It also comprehends much more than the soul's personal relationship with God. It has a social, even a political, dimension.

Furthermore there is no single mode or style of spirituality for Christians. Each of us must adapt the call to perfection to his or her own identity and situation. What will always be common to each is love of God and love of neighbor. "For charity, as the bond of perfection and the fulfillment of the law (cf. Col. 3:14; Rom. 13:10), rules over all the means of attaining holiness, gives life to them, and makes them work. Hence it is the love of God and of neighbor which points out the true disciple of Christ" (Dogmatic Constitution on the Church, n. 42).

Elsewhere the council reaffirms or elaborates upon these basic principles of Christian spirituality. The call to holiness is a call issued to laity as well as to clergy and religious. According to the Decree on the Apostolate of the Laity, their spiritual life will be rooted in the mysteries of creation and redemption, in the presence of the Holy Spirit, and in the mission of Christ and the Church (n. 29).

The Christian enters upon the spiritual life in response to the Word of God (Dogmatic Constitution on Divine Revelation, n. 21), and this in turn is proclaimed and celebrated in the liturgy of the Church, which is the "summit" and the "fountain" of the whole Christian life: "From the liturgy, therefore, and especially from the Eucharist, as from a fountain, grace is channeled into us; and our sanctification in Christ and the glorification of God, to which all other activities of the Church are directed as toward their goal, are most powerfully achieved" (Constitution on the Sacred Liturgy, n. 10).

And what the council taught about Catholic spirituality applies to the whole Body of Christ: "Let all Christ's faithful remember that the more purely they strive to live according to the gospel, the more they are fostering and even practicing Christian unity" (Decree on Ecumenism, n. 7). The more all Christians "enjoy profound communion with the Father, the Word, and the Spirit," the more surely will they "achieve depth and ease in strengthening mutual brotherhood [and sisterhood]." The council insisted that this is, in fact, "the soul of the whole ecumenical movement, and can rightly be called 'spiritual ecumenism.'" Indeed "there can be no ecumenism worthy of the name without a change of heart," that is, without *conversion* (Decree on Ecumenism, n. 7).

CONVERSION

If one is to understand what spirituality is all about and what it has to do with the Church and its ministries, one has to reflect more deliberately on this fundamental notion of conversion, to which the Second Vatican Council refers, and also on the Kingdom of God, to which conversion is ultimately directed.

Both these concepts come together in a definition of the

Church. The Church is a community of disciples, that is, of those who have been converted and who are on the way to the fullness of the Kingdom of God. The mission of the Church is not only to proclaim, celebrate, and serve that Kingdom but to be a credible sign of it by really acting like a community of converts.

A *convert* is a person who has moved to a different level of human consciousness. The Christian convert is one who believes in Jesus Christ and whose whole life is determined by that belief. The process by which a person moves to that new level of consciousness is called conversion. More precisely it is Christian conversion, since conversion to God is an invitation and possibility for every human being. I am referring here to conversion to God in Jesus Christ.

The call of Jesus was a call to repentance and faith, to a change of mind, or of consciousness, and to a new mode of behavior in keeping with that change of mind. We are to live according to the new demands of the Kingdom of God. We are to make God the center and active source of our whole being. We are to be transformed ourselves by the redemptive, healing presence of God and then to allow God to work through us to redeem and heal others and the whole world, enemies as well as friends, the outcasts as well as the respectable, the poor as well as the rich, the sinners as well as the righteous.

The whole of Jesus' preaching is summed up by Mark: "This is the time of fulfillment. The kingdom of God is at hand. Repent, and believe in the gospel" (1:15). Thus his preaching is at once a proclamation and a warning. It announces a divine act (the coming of the Kingdom of God) and demands a response from us (conversion). The Kingdom calls forth conversion.

Jesus' preaching of the Kingdom of God was frequently couched in parables in which he often inverted his listeners' whole worldview. Thus the parable of the Good Samaritan (Luke 10:25–37) is not simply an example of neighborliness. If that were all Jesus wanted to communicate—that we are called to be the neighbor to one in need—he would have made the Samaritan the injured party and the Israelite the one who came along to aid him. No Jew of the time would ever have expected hospitality from a Samaritan (see Luke 9:52–56). Thus the parable challenges the listener to conceive the inconceivable—the Samaritan is "good"—and to reexamine his or her most basic social attitudes and values. The parable is no longer merely instruction; it is proclamation itself.

For Jesus nothing is more precious than the Kingdom of God, that is, the healing and renewing presence and activity of God on our behalf. Instead, "seek his kingdom, and these other things will be given you besides" (Luke 12:31). Like a person who finds a hidden treasure in a field or a merchant who discovers a precious pearl, we must be prepared to give up everything else in order to possess the Kingdom (Matt. 13:44–46).

But the Kingdom is promised only to those with a certain outlook and way of life (see the Beatitudes in Matt. 5:3–8). One can inherit the Kingdom through love of one's neighbor (Matt. 25:34–40), and yet one must also accept it as a child, that is, as one without power (Matt. 10:15).

Jesus assured the scribe who grasped the meaning of the

chief of the commandments (love of God and love of neighbor): "You are not far from the kingdom of God" (Mark 12:34). He also insisted to his disciples that their commitment to the Kingdom would make strong demands upon them (Mark 10:1; Luke 9:57–62; Matt. 19:12).

Conversion, therefore, has at least two components—repentance and faith. And both are directed to the coming Kingdom of God. Jesus calls us, first, to repentance (*metanoia*, a change of mind). To the Semite *metanoia* meant a turning away from one's former consciousness, now recognized as wrong, and a striking out in a completely new direction. *Metanoia*, embracing conversion and repentance together, is not just sorrow for sin but a fundamental reorientation of one's whole life. Jesus demanded that his listeners not only repent but also believe the gospel of forgiveness that he preached (Mark 2:10, 17). And he drove home his point with various parables, especially those in Luke 15 and the parable of the prodigal son in particular.

Jesus was so committed to the forgiveness of sins in the name of God that he made himself the friend of outcasts such as publicans and sinners and did not avoid their company (Matt. 11:19; Mark 2:16). Indeed he rejoiced over their conversion (Luke 15:7–10; Matt. 18:13).

The antithesis of a repentant attitude, then as now, is an attitude of self-righteousness and presumption. Jesus repudiated the proud Pharisee (Luke 18:10–14), the elder brother who resented his father's benevolent reaction to the prodigal son's return (Luke 15:25–32), and the discontented laborers in the vineyard (Matt. 20:1–15). To those who set themselves proudly above others, Jesus declared that publicans and harlots would enter the Kingdom before they would (Matt. 21:31–32). He condemned pompous religious leaders for trying to shut the doors of the Kingdom (Matt. 23:13). All of us, he warned, are unprofitable servants (Luke 17:10), ever in God's debt (Matt. 6:12). God will exalt the humble and bring down the proud (Luke 14:11; 18:14). We must pray that God forgives our trespasses. And only those who are without sin should cast the first stone (John 8:7).

The early Church would continue this message: "Repent and be baptized . . . " (Acts 2:38). Repentance, therefore, remains a major element of Christian spirituality, even if not the central element.

Jesus also demanded faith, which is the positive side of conversion (Mark 1:15). He said to the woman who had been afflicted with a hemorrhage for a dozen years and who was cured by touching his clothing, "Daughter, your faith has saved you" (Luke 8:48). From there he went to the house of the official whose daughter was reported as being already dead. Jesus disregarded the report and said to the official, "Do not be afraid; just have faith and she will be saved" (Luke 8:50).

It was the faith of the lame man's friends that called forth from Jesus the forgiveness of his sins and physical healing (Mark 2:5). Faith is also central to the narrative of the cured boy in Mark 9:14–29. Jesus sighed over this unbelieving generation (Mark 9:19) and reminded the boy's father that all things are possible to him who believes (Mark 9:23).

Moved by the great faith of the Syro-Phoenician woman, Jesus healed her daughter (Mark 7:26–30), and he drew attention to the faith of the pagan centurion who believed that a mere word from Jesus would heal his sick servant (Matt. 8:10; Luke 7:9). On the other hand, where Jesus encountered an obstinate lack of faith, he was not able to manifest the signs of salvation (Mark 6:5–6).

This, of course, is a broader and more profound understanding of conversion than had been traditionally proposed since the Council of Trent, with that council's necessary emphasis on the intellectual and objective character of faith. According to post-Tridentine neo-Scholastic theology (the theology that informs our pre-Vatican II catechisms and seminary textbooks), to be converted was to accept divine revelation as authoritatively presented by the Church.

A convert was not defined primarily as one who had had a radical "change of mind" and who had opened himself or herself to God's Kingdom but rather as one who had decided to "enter the Catholic Church." Whether one had previously been a committed Lutheran, a Buddhist, or an atheist did not essentially matter. A convert was a non-Catholic who had become a Catholic.

The determining feature of conversion, therefore, was ecclesiastical (that is, accepting the claims of a Church) rather than Christological or eschatological (that is, accepting the call of Jesus Christ to the Kingdom of God). Conversion had to do with one's new relationship to the Catholic Church rather than with one's new self-understanding in relationship to God, to Jesus Christ, and to the Kingdom.

We passed from this neo-Scholastic, classicist understanding of conversion to an historically conscious notion of conversion around the time of the Second Vatican Council. To use the language of the late Jesuit theologian Bernard

Lonergan, conversion came to mean a shifting of horizons (*Method in Theology* [New York: Herder and Herder, 1972], pp. 235–244). An horizon is that which circumscribes or sets limits to a person's interests and knowledge. Beyond one's horizons are matters that are neither known nor cared about.

A conversion is a radical transformation from which follows on all levels of life an interlocking series of changes and developments. What had once gone unnoticed becomes vivid and present. What had once been of no concern is now of the highest importance. There is a change in oneself, in one's relations with others, and in one's relation to God. Conversion, then, is the transformation of the individual and of his or her world. One's direction is altered, one's eyes are opened, and one perceives the world in a new way. Indeed one perceives a new world, the Kingdom of God.

To see a new world, that is, to see the Kingdom, is to enter a new form of existence, one rooted in the spirit rather than the flesh. One is intent now on the things of the spirit because one lives now "according to the spirit" (Rom. 8:5). But every conversion is only a beginning. Indeed in the Rite of Christian Initiation of Adults it is only the first of several stages leading to baptism and then postbaptismal catechesis, or *mystagogia*.

Conversion is both act and process, once-and-for-all and ongoing. The final test of conversion is whether or not it leads to and is continually expressed in love for the neighbor. As John's first epistle states it: "If anyone says, 'I love God,' but hates his brother [or his sister], he is a liar; for whoever does not love a brother [or a sister] whom he has seen cannot love God whom he has not seen. This is the commandment we have from him: whoever loves God must also love his brother [and his sister]" (1 John 4:20–21). And those who so love their neighbor will enter the Kingdom, for as often as we do it to one of these, the least of his brethren, we do it to him (Matt. 25:40).

SOME CRITERIA FOR EVALUATING SPIRITUALITIES

Spirituality is a general term, like religion. There is no such thing as "religion in general." There are specific religions: Christianity, Judaism, and so forth. Likewise, there is no such thing as "spirituality in general." There are spiritualities: Christian, Buddhist, and so forth.

And just as there are subdivisions within individual religions (Christianity is composed of Catholicism, Protestantism, Anglicanism, Eastern Orthodoxy, and so forth), so, too, are there subdivisions within Christian spirituality: Dominican, Franciscan, Benedictine, Ignatian, and so forth. Today many new forms of spirituality, not tied to religious orders as older forms have been, vie for our attention and engagement.

How is the Church's minister to decide which of these spiritualities offers a genuinely catholic style of Christian life? How is the Church's minister to discern the problems and difficulties that one finds in some spiritualities today?

The following criteria will help each minister and potential minister make these judgments:

1. Christian spirituality is holistic.
2. Christian spirituality is other-oriented.
3. Christian spirituality is pluralistic.
4. Christian spirituality is humane.
5. Christian spirituality is trinitarian.
6. Christian spirituality is sacramental.
7. Christian spirituality is Kingdom-oriented.
8. Christian spirituality is sacrificial.
9. Christian spirituality is ecclesial, or Church-oriented.
10. Christian spirituality is for all Christians.

Holistic Spirituality

We are neither purely bodily creatures nor purely spiritual. Nor are we even primarily one or the other. We are body-spirits.

The spirit-flesh opposition we find in St. Paul is not an opposition between our bodies and our souls. It is an opposition between our whole person as oriented, on the one hand, toward the Kingdom of God, and our whole person as oriented, on the other hand, away from God in the pursuit of selfish interests. Christians who misread the spirit-flesh opposition in Paul tend to favor spiritualities that depreciate the body, human emotions, human passions, social relationships, our material environment, and the like. They act as if we are not really body-spirits but spirits imprisoned in our bodies, waiting always to be released from this "vale of tears."

A spirituality that depreciates the body is a spirituality that, in effect, denies the work of the triune God as creator, redeemer, and sanctifier. We have a bodily existence because God created us that way. Although we have sinned in bodily ways, our bodily existence has been raised to even greater levels by the incarnation of the Word. And through the sending of the Holy Spirit, we are constantly energized and renewed by the ongoing presence of God within us.

But, of course, we are not *only* bodily creatures. Indeed a "spirituality" that exalted the body at the expense of the spirit would be a contradiction in terms. That criticism applies to many of the so-called "human potential movements" that have sprung up in the last few decades. Ministry is not for the sake of personal fulfillment or material gratification. It exists always for the service of others—in their bodily as well as their spiritual needs. In other words, just as the minister is a body-spirit, so are those whom the minister serves body-spirits. Ministerial spirituality, therefore, must be *holistic*, not dualistic.

Other-Oriented Spirituality

We are radically social beings. Accordingly no authentically Christian spirituality can attend exclusively or in an exaggerated fashion to the individual's personal relationship with God, with Jesus, or with the Holy Spirit as if other persons and the wider created order did not enter intrinsically into those relationships. Our spirituality must open us to others, not close us off from them. An inability to relate to others, therefore, is *never* a sign of personal intimacy with God, who is present in others.

Why was it ever said, for example, that "it's impossible to live with a saint"? Is it because people used to identify holiness with oddness? Because sitting at table with a saint means never telling a joke that might be even slightly off-color? Because having a saint as a collaborator in ministry means being forced to pray interminably at the strangest times? Because being married to a saint means never looking at or touching the saint with passion?

All this, of course, is nonsense. Holiness is not oddness. Holiness is wholeness. It should be difficult to live or work with a saint only if the saint reminds us of our own failure to live up to the highest standards of the gospel, namely, love of God and love of neighbor.

Saints, therefore, are people of virtue. They are people of faith, hope, and love. They are people of prudence, justice, temperance, and fortitude. They are people of mercy and compassion. And they have an exquisite sense of humor because they really do see the great discrepancy between our finite human pretensions and the grandeur of the Kingdom that the Lord has promised us. To be a saint is to love God in the other. Consequently, ministerial spirituality must be *other-oriented*, not individualistic.

Pluralistic Spirituality

We are social beings, it is true, but we are also individuals, distinct centers of consciousness and freedom. Accordingly no authentically Christian spirituality can allow the individual to be absorbed into some impersonal collective.

No religious order, no school of spirituality, no ecclesiastical movement, no special group of Christians has a monopoly on holiness. There is a wide variety of possibilities for developing a Christian spirituality because there is no single way of experiencing God or of expressing the experience of God in our lives.

Consequently no single form of spirituality may be imposed on a whole group of Christians, ministers included. Each individual has to have the freedom to cultivate his or her own personal relationship with God, but always in the context of the Church at large and the particular community of faith with which the believer is associated.

There is a balance, then, to be struck. No spirituality should be so individualized that it becomes idiosyncratic, unrecognizable even to those who are known and respected for their wisdom, fair-mindedness, and common sense. But neither should any spirituality be so monolithic that individuals who cannot embrace it are subject to censure and reproach, directly or indirectly, overtly or subtly.

Thus there is no one priestly spirituality that every priest must adopt. Neither is there one spirituality for religious women and men, for religious educators, or for youth ministers. "Hence, let there be unity in what is necessary, freedom in what is unsettled, and charity in any case" (Pastoral Constitution on the Church in the Modern World, n. 92). Ministerial spirituality is *pluralistic*, not monolithic.

Humane Spirituality

We are graced. God is present and active within us. In fact, God's presence enters into the very definition of what it means to be human. The doctrines of creation and redemption make it impossible for the Christian to reject the material, the fleshly, the bodily, the natural, the tangible, the visible, the historical, the concrete.

No authentically Christian spirituality, therefore, can legitimately endorse a repression of the human or dismiss whole components of human existence (for example, the passions, or the so-called lower appetites) as if they were somehow dishonorable and bestial.

There is such a thing as Christian humanism, to which great saints like Thomas More (d. 1535) and Catherine of Siena (d. 1380) have given luminous witness. To be indifferent or even hostile to the human is to be indifferent to the God who created and sustains us, to the Christ who became flesh with us and redeemed us, and to the Holy Spirit who renews us and draws us closer to one another and to God. Ministerial spirituality, therefore, is *humane*, not antihuman.

Trinitarian Spirituality

To be graced is to be alive by a principle that transcends us, namely, the presence of God. For the Christian, however, God is triune. Christian spirituality, therefore, is trinitarian, not unitarian.

We are created, called, and sustained by the Father, redeemed and recreated by the Son, and renewed and empowered to live a fully human life by the Holy Spirit. Therefore, spirituality is not authentically Christian if it seeks to fashion a relationship with God the Father alone, with God the Son alone, or with God the Holy Spirit alone.

A unitarianism of the first divine person leaves us with a remote God who created us but who remains essentially distant from our existence and from our undertakings. It was in the United States that classical Unitarianism (that is, a unitarianism of the first divine person) initially took root, and it continues to be reinforced in much of our culture. It conveys the idea of God "up there in the sky," to whom we pay lip service on special occasions and who leaves us pretty much alone to pursue our own human ends.

A unitarianism of the second divine person leaves us with a brother-God who walks with us and shares our human condition, but who doesn't call us beyond ourselves and beyond our history. Some of the so-called death-of-God theologians of the 1960s adopted this view; God is Jesus, and Jesus is the "man for others" who stands alongside us in the service of the brethren who are in need.

A unitarianism of the third divine person leaves us with a Spirit who is unconnected with any particular historical events (including especially *the* event of the Incarnation). It is no accident that many charismatic Christians often show little or no interest in public affairs. For them history seems essentially unimportant. Only the present experience of the Spirit matters.

Ministerial spirituality, therefore, is *trinitarian*, not unitarian.

Sacramental Spirituality

Since the triune God is present and active everywhere, all reality—personal, natural, historical, cosmic—has a sacramental character. The invisible God is embodied in and mediated by visible realities.

Therefore the horizon or scope of Christian spirituality will always be as wide as the created order itself. It will be as worldly—in the best sense of the word—as it is personal. In other words, it will strive always to see God in all things, as St. Ignatius Loyola said so insistently.

An authentically Christian spirituality will not be closed off from important components of human reality: art, politics, science, and even play, as well as worship and prayer. Everything offers the possibility of an encounter with God, for God is present to everything.

Accordingly ministerial spirituality will be celebrative and eucharistic. It will never tire of searching God's creation and of plumbing the depths of one's own experiences, for God is always to be found there. Ministerial spirituality is *sacramental*, not unidimensional.

Kingdom-oriented Spirituality

Humankind and the world in which we live are destined for and therefore oriented toward the Kingdom of God. But the Kingdom of God, as we pointed out in chapter 1, is a kingdom of justice and peace as well as of holiness and grace. An authentically Christian spirituality will always be responsive to the demands of justice, of peace, and of human rights, and will never be closed off from or indifferent to the needs and the cries of the poor and the oppressed.

Justice is a cardinal virtue. To lack it is to lack something essential to Christian holiness. Concern for the poor and for the socially marginalized was at the center of Jesus' preaching and ministry. In fact, when confronted by the disciples of John the Baptist, he cited this as the sign by which his mission could be authenticated. "Go and tell John what you hear and see: the blind regain their sight, the lame walk, lepers are cleansed, the deaf hear, the dead are raised, and the poor have the good news proclaimed to them" (Matt. 11:4–5).

Jesus himself has set the standard for his Church's ministers. Let them minister as he ministered. Let them cultivate a style of spiritual life oriented to the Kingdom of God, not one turned in upon itself and insensitive to the legitimate claims of the poor and oppressed. Let them not confuse attention to religious duties—rituals, laws, traditions, and customs—with the service of God. Ministerial spirituality, therefore, is *Kingdom-oriented*, not religion-oriented.

Sacrificial Spirituality

We are graced, but we are also sinners. There can be no authentically Christian spirituality apart from the Cross. Christian spirituality, therefore, is always marked by sacrifice, denial of selfish interests, even contradictions. It is mindful always of the impact of Original Sin: of pride, apathy, temerity, lust, hypocrisy, sloth, and the like.

The Christian knows, as a Christian, that there is no Easter without Good Friday. "Amen, amen, I say to you, unless a grain of wheat falls to the ground and dies, it remains just a grain of wheat; but if it dies, it produces much fruit" (John 12:24). The Christian also knows, as a human being, that there is no love without cost. Love by its nature is sacrificial. It gives to the other without calculation. It seeks only the well-being of the other.

Married Christians who have raised a family know exactly what this means. This is not textbook spirituality. It is what life is all about. Just as we love sacrificially within the family, so we must be prepared to love sacrificially within the larger family of the Church and beyond that within the still larger human family.

A sacrificial spirituality, therefore, will be rooted in the theological virtues (faith, hope, and love) and moral virtues (prudence, justice, temperance, and fortitude). Its center, however, will always be love. For sacrifice without love is empty. Ministerial spirituality is *sacrificial*, not selfish.

Ecclesial, or Church-oriented, Spirituality

We are ecclesial persons. Our Christian faith comes in the first instance from the Church's proclamation of the Word of God, is ratified in baptism and confirmation, is celebrated again and again in the Eucharist, and is otherwise nurtured and sustained within the faith community itself.

There is no authentically Christian spirituality apart from the life of the Church and especially apart from its life of worship. Vatican II's Constitution on the Sacred Liturgy declared that the Eucharist is the summit and the source of the whole Christian life (n. 10). A Christian spirituality that does not place the Eucharist at its center is inauthentically Christian.

But the Eucharist is only the most important act of the *Church*. It is the Church that is at worship in the Eucharist. It is the Church that proclaims the Word of God. It is the Church that calls people to mission for the sake of the Kingdom of God.

A ministerial spirituality, therefore, must be ecclesiologically balanced. It must reflect the totality of the Church's *nature* as a community, an institution, and a mystery, and it must reflect the totality of the Church's *mission* of word, worship, witness, and service. Ministerial spirituality is indeed *ecclesial*, not atomistic or individualistic.

Spirituality for All Christians

The call to Christian holiness is a universal call (Dogmatic Constitution on the Church, chapter 5). There is no "higher" spirituality for the ordained and the religiously professed, nor is there a "lower" spirituality for the laity. The whole Church is the People of God, and the whole Church is called to holiness. Christian spirituality, therefore, is never hierarchical or elitist. "Thus it is evident to everyone that the faithful of Christ of whatever rank or status are called to the fullness of the Christian life and to the perfection of charity. . . . All of Christ's followers, therefore, are invited and bound to pursue holiness and the perfect fulfillment of their proper state" (Dogmatic Constitution on the Church, nn. 40, 42).

Christian spirituality, therefore, is rooted in baptism and confirmation, not in ordination or in religious profession. For that reason, Christian spirituality is *for all Christians*, and that includes, of course, all the Church's ministers, not just priests, nuns, and monks.

SUMMARY

1.   Christian ministers are *signs* as well as instruments of grace. As such, they must personally witness to what they proclaim and provide to others. That means ministering with believing love and loving faith.

2.   Christian spirituality is a style of life that flows from the presence of the Spirit within us and within the Church. It is a matter of living in accordance with who we have become in the Spirit and of manifesting the fruits of the Spirit's presence: mercy, kindness, patience, and so forth.

3.   Christian spirituality begins with conversion and reaches its culmination in the Kingdom of God.

4.   A convert is one who believes in Jesus Christ and whose whole life is determined by that belief. As such, conversion requires repentance and faith—a turning away from one's former self to a new life in Christ.

5.   Conversion, however, is not a once-and-for-all event. It is a process. We are always on the way to perfection and the Kingdom of God. In the meantime the measure of our progress is our love of neighbor.

6.   There are ten criteria by which to discern among competing spiritualities:

- Christian spirituality is holistic (we are body-spirits), not dualistic (body versus spirit).
- Christian spirituality is other-oriented, not individualistic.
- Christian spirituality is pluralistic, not monolithic. There is no single spirituality for all Christians, nor even for all in a particular group or class of Christians.
- Christian spirituality is humane, not antihuman. It embraces whatever God has created and redeemed.
- Christian spirituality is trinitarian, not unitarian.
- Christian spirituality is sacramental, not unidimensional. It sees God in all things.

- Christian spirituality is Kingdom-oriented, not religion-oriented.
- Christian spirituality is sacrificial, not self-centered or narcissistic.
- Christian spirituality is Church-oriented, not atomistic or individualistic.
- Christian spirituality is for all Christians, not for monks, priests, and nuns alone.

DISCUSSION QUESTIONS

1. "The bishop is a very spiritual man. Indeed he's a holy priest." What do you think people really mean when they say things like that? In light of your understanding of theology, doctrine, and sacred Scripture, how would you describe a truly holy, or spiritual, Christian?

2. That ministers must personally embody what they proclaim is a textbookish statement. Can you verify this from your own experience? Can you cite a case or two of people who have ministered to you or to your family and friends? How did the minister's personal witness enter into the act of ministry itself?

3. From what you know of the charismatic movement in the Catholic Church and the Pentecostal and "born-again" movements in some of the Protestant churches, would you actively encourage or discourage Christians influenced by those movements to minister in your parish? Explain.

4. Which of the ten criteria for spirituality do you think are

most often violated in the Church as you know it today? Which of the ten criteria seem to be most frequently honored? Can you think of other criteria that might be useful in helping you and others to discern authentic from inauthentic Christian spiritualities?

5.   There is to be a grand commissioning service in the diocesan cathedral. More than a hundred so-called lay ministers from all over the diocese are being sent out as youth ministers, eucharistic ministers, ministers to the sick and handicapped, religious educators, and the like. The bishop has invited you to give the homily. What points would you want to get across to the congregation?

6.   Having a vibrant ministerial spirituality is easier said than done. If you were appointed diocesan spiritual director (a mythical post, of course), how would you go about reaching ministers at all levels: presbyters, deacons, religious educators, youth ministers, college chaplains, hospital chaplains, ministers to the elderly, social ministers, and so forth?

7.   You're on duty in the parish office one day, and someone comes to the door. The person acts a bit self-conscious but is obviously intelligent and serious. First comes a question: "How do I go about becoming a minister in the parish?" Before you can even begin to answer, the person adds a request: "I'd need someone to help me grow spiritually so that my ministry here would be as fruitful as possible." Could you offer such a person any help? Where would you begin?

SUGGESTED READINGS

Brueggemann, Walter, Sharon Parks, and Thomas H. Groome. *To Act Justly, Love Tenderly, Walk Humbly: An Agenda for Ministers*. New York: Paulist Press, 1986. The authors represent a broad spectrum of expertise: an Old Testament scholar, a psychologist of religion, and a religious educator.

Chittister, Joan. *Women, Ministry and the Church*. New York: Paulist Press, 1983. A collection of essays on the roles and problems of women in the ministries of today's Church, by one of the nation's most respected Church leaders.

Coll, Regina, ed. *Women and Religion: A Reader for Clergy*. New York: Paulist Press, 1982. Described by the editor as "an attempt to bridge the gap . . . between women who have newly found their voices and men who are trying to open their ears," this book speaks frankly of the patriarchalism and clericalism that continue to affect the exercise of ministry in the Church.

Cowan, Michael A., ed. *Alternative Futures for Worship*. Vol. 6, *Leadership Ministry in Community*. Collegeville, MN: The Liturgical Press, 1987. Useful essays, emphasizing the spiritual dimension of ministry, by James and Evelyn Whitehead, David Power, John Shea, and the editor.

Doohan, Leonard. *The Lay-Centered Church: Theology and Spirituality*. San Francisco: Harper & Row, 1984. While the entire book is of value for all ministers and ministerial candidates, chapter 4, "Spirituality of All the Baptized," is especially pertinent.

Metz, Johannes B. *Followers of Christ: The Religious Life and the Church*. New York: Paulist Press, 1978. An excellent little book on religious life, with application for those outside as well as in religious communities. Metz is especially good on the evangelical counsels: poverty, celibacy, and obedience.

Power, David. *Gifts That Differ: Lay Ministries Established and Un-*

established. New York: Pueblo, 1985. Contains a survey of lay ministries that have appeared in the last few decades, situating them in their wider historical context.

Rahner, Karl. *The Church and the Sacraments*. New York: Herder, 1963. The material on Holy Order is especially pertinent (pp. 95–106), but the whole book is a major statement on the sacraments.

POSTSCRIPT

This book has been about the high calling of Church ministry. It has focused often on the qualifications, standards, and responsibilities each minister must meet.

Because the minister is a servant of the Church, the Church has both the duty and the right to subject its ministers to careful scrutiny. Each minister must demonstrate a capacity and a readiness to serve the People of God effectively.

But responsibility is a two-way street. Not only do ministers have obligations toward the Church but the Church also has obligations toward its ministers. "While the Church is bound to give witness to justice," declared the Third International Synod of Bishops' *Justice in the World* (1971), "it recognizes that anyone who ventures to speak to people about justice must first be just in their eyes . . . . Within the Church rights must be preserved. No one should be deprived of his [or her] ordinary rights because he [or she] is associated with the Church in one way or another. Those who serve the Church by their labor, including priests and religious, should receive a sufficient livelihood and enjoy that social security which is customary in their region."

The United States Catholic bishops' pastoral letter, *Economic Justice for All: Catholic Social Teaching and the U.S. Economy* (1986), draws upon the same synodal document and applies it forcefully to the Church in the United States. Paragraph 351 is so important that it merits quotation in full:

> We bishops commit ourselves to the principle that those who serve the church—laity, clergy and religious—should receive a sufficient livelihood and the social benefits provided by responsible employers in our nation. These obligations, however, cannot be met without the increased contributions of all the members of the church. We call on all to recognize their responsibility to contribute monetarily to the support of those who carry out the public mission of the church. Sacrificial giving or tithing by all the people of God would provide the funds necessary to pay these adequate salaries for religious and lay people; the lack of funds is the usual underlying cause for the lack of adequate salaries. The obligation to sustain the church's institutions—education and health care, social service agencies, religious education programs, care of the elderly, youth ministry and the like—falls on all the members of the community because of their baptism; the obligation is not just on the users or on those who staff them. Increased resources are also needed for the support of elderly members of religious communities. These dedicated women and men have not always asked for or received the stipends and pensions that would have assured their future. It would be a breach of our obligations to them to let them or their communities face retirement without adequate funds.

Sometimes bishops and other ecclesiastical officials resist the attempts of diocesan and parish ministers to form associations that would ensure the ministers' individual and collective rights. The United States bishops' pastoral letter stands with those who work for the Church: "All church institutions must also fully recognize the rights of employees to organize and bargain collectively with the institution through whatever association or organization they freely choose" (para. 353).

And then, of course, there is the age-old problem of discrimination, direct or indirect, blatant or hidden, based on sex. The bishops also take a firm stand on justice toward women in the Church:

> In seeking greater justice in wages, we recognize the need to be particularly alert to the continuing discrimination against women throughout church and society, especially reflected in both the inequities of salaries between women and men and in the concentration of women in jobs at the lower end of the wage scale. (para. 353)

It all comes down once more to sacramentality. The Church is at once a sign and an instrument of the Kingdom of God. The Church's effectiveness as an instrument, however, is dependent upon its credibility as a sign. "The authenticity of that sign," the United States Catholic bishops insisted in their 1980 pastoral document *Called and Gifted*, "depends on all the people: laity, religious, deacons, priests, and bishops. Unless we truly live as the People of God, we will not be much of a sign to ourselves or to the world."

We all have our work cut out for us.

Appendix:

CALLED AND GIFTED: THE AMERICAN CATHOLIC LAITY

Reflections of the American Bishops Commemorating the Fifteenth Anniversary of the Issuance of the *Decree on the Apostolate of the Laity*

NATIONAL CONFERENCE OF CATHOLIC BISHOPS

INTRODUCTION

Among the most enduring contributions of the Second Vatican Council is its description of the Church as the People of God. "This was to be the new People of God. For, those who believe in Christ, who are reborn not from a perishable but from an imperishable seed through the Word of the living God (I Pet. 1:23), not from the flesh but from water and the Holy Spirit (Jn. 3:5–6), are finally established as 'a chosen race, a royal priesthood, a holy nation, a purchased people . . . You who in times past were not a people, but are now the people of God.'" (I Pet. 2:9–10). (*Lumen Gentium*, #9)

This image, drawing on a rich biblical and historical tradition, gives marvelous expression to the role of the Church as the sign of the Kingdom of God. It was this Kingdom which Jesus came to announce and to inaugurate by his life, death, and resurrection. "After John's arrest, Jesus appeared in Galilee proclaiming the good news of God. 'This is the time of fulfillment. The reign of God is at hand. Reform your lives and believe in the gospel.' " (Mk. 1:14–16)

Jesus established the Church to bear witness to God's Kingdom especially by the way his followers would live as the People of God. "This is my commandment: love one another as I have loved you." (Jn. 15:12)

The image of the People of God has many dimensions; its meaning is best grasped through a variety of experiences. Each sheds light on the whole and enables us to appreciate and live it more deeply.

At the present time the light shed on the meaning of the People of God by the laity is especially noteworthy and exciting. In an exercise of our charism of "bringing forth from the treasury of Revelation new things and old" (*Lumen Gentium*, #25), we bishops praise the Lord for what is happening among the laity and proclaim as well as we can what we have been experiencing and learning from them.

While focusing on the laity, we wish to address the whole Church. We affirm the vision of the Second Vatican Council and the importance it gives to the laity. We look forward to what is still to come under the guidance of the Holy Spirit, making the Church more and more the perfect image of Christ. We also acknowledge that these continuing developments may require new concepts, new terminology, new attitudes, and new practices. In prayerful dialogue with all our sisters and brothers we are prepared to make those changes which will aid in building the Kingdom.

THE CALL TO ADULTHOOD

As the *Decree on the Apostolate of the Laity* of Vatican II says:

Indeed, everyone should painstakingly ready himself or herself personally for the apostolate, especially as an adult. For the advance of age brings with it better self-knowledge, thus enabling each person to evaluate more accurately the talents with which God has enriched each soul and to exercise more effectively those charismatic gifts which the Holy Spirit has bestowed on all for the good of others. (#30)

One of the chief characteristics of lay men and women today is their growing sense of being adult members of the Church. Adulthood implies knowledge, experience and awareness, freedom and responsibility, and mutuality in relationships. It is true, however, that the experience of lay persons "as Church members" has not always reflected this understanding of adulthood. Now, thanks to the impetus of the Second Vatican Council, lay women and men feel themselves called to exercise the same mature interdependence and practical self-direction which characterize them in other areas of life.

We note the response of many lay persons to different opportunities for faith development. There is the "coming to faith in Jesus" and a strengthening of commitment to Him and His mission which we commonly call evangelization. There is also the adult catechesis movement which allows persons to grow and deepen their faith, and there are those who in faith are seeking greater understanding through theological reflection. These and other adult lay persons have taken responsibility in their parish or diocese by serving in leadership positions on committees and boards.

Adult Christian living is also noticeable, though not always as publicized, in the daily struggle to live out Christian values in family, neighborhood, school, government, and work. This is a hopeful sign because the laity are uniquely present in and to the world and so bear a privileged position to build the Kingdom of God there. "You are the light of the world . . . Your light must shine before all so that they may see goodness in your acts and give praise to your heavenly Father." (Mt. 5:14–16)

The adult character of the People of God flows from baptism and confirmation which are the foundation of the Christian life and ministry. They signify initiation into a community of believers who, according to their state of life, respond to God's call to holiness and accept responsibility for the ministry of the Church.

THE CALL TO HOLINESS

Thus it is evident to everyone that all the faithful of Christ of whatever rank or status are called to the fullness of the Christian life and to the perfection of charity. By this holiness a more human way of life is promoted even in this earthly society. (*Lumen Gentium*, #40)

The Second Vatican Council clearly proclaimed the universal call to holiness. Not only are lay people included in

God's call to holiness, but theirs is a unique call requiring a unique response which itself is a gift of the Holy Spirit. It is characteristic that lay men and women hear the call to holiness in the very web of their existence (*Lumen Gentium*, #31), in and through the events of the world, the pluralism of modern living, the complex decisions and conflicting values they must struggle with, the richness and fragility of sexual relationships, the delicate balance between activity and stillness, presence and privacy, love and loss.

The response of lay people to this call promises to contribute still more to the spiritual heritage of the Church. Already the laity's hunger for God's word is everywhere evident. Increasingly, lay men and women are seeking spiritual formation and direction in deep ways of prayer. This has helped to spur several renewal movements.

These developments present a challenge to the parish because, for the most part, the spiritual needs of lay people must be met in the parish. The parish must be a home where they can come together with their leaders for mutual spiritual enrichment, much as in the early Church: "They devoted themselves to the apostles' instruction and the communal life, to the breaking of bread and the prayers" (Acts. 2:42).

We call special attention to the effect this should have on liturgy. The quality of worship depends in great measure on the spiritual life of all present. As lay women and men cultivate their own proper response to God's call to holiness, this should come to expression in the communal worship of the Church.

Simultaneously, as lay persons assume their roles in liturgical celebration according to the gifts of the Spirit bestowed on them for that purpose, the ordained celebrant will be more clearly seen as the one who presides over the community, bringing together the diverse talents of the community as a gift to the Father.

Whatever else the growing spiritual life of the community entails, it certainly means a more intense sharing among the whole People of God of the gifts of the Spirit. And this we wish to reinforce.

THE CALL TO MINISTRY

From the reception of these charisms or gifts, including those which are less dramatic, there arise for each believer the right and duty to use them in the Church and the world for the good of humankind and for the upbuilding of the Church. (*Decree on the Apostolate of the Laity*, #3)

Baptism and confirmation empower all believers to share in some form of ministry. Although the specific form of participation in ministry varies according to the gifts of the Holy Spirit, all who share in this work are united with one another. "Just as each of us has one body with many members, and not all the members have the same function, so too we, though many, are one body in Christ and individually members of one another. We have gifts that differ according to the favor bestowed on each of us." (Rom. 12:4–6)

This unity in the ministry should be especially evident in the relationships between laity and clergy as lay men and women respond to the call of the Spirit in their lives. The clergy help to call forth, identify, coordinate, and affirm the diverse gifts bestowed by the Spirit. We applaud this solidarity between laity and clergy as their most effective ministry and witness to the world.

CHRISTIAN SERVICE:
MINISTRY IN THE WORLD

The laity, by their vocation, seek the Kingdom of God by engaging in temporal affairs, and by ordering them according to the plan of God. (*Lumen Gentium,* #31)

Christian service in the world is represented in a preeminent way by the laity. It is sometimes called the "ministry of the laity" and balances the concept of ministry found in the ecclesial ministerial services. Because of lay persons, Christian service or ministry broadly understood includes civic and public activity, response to the imperatives of peace and justice, and resolution of social, political, and economic conflicts, especially as they influence the poor, oppressed and minorities.

The whole Church faces unprecedented situations in the contemporary world, and lay people are at the cutting edge of these new challenges. It is they who engage directly in the task of relating Christian values and practices to complex questions such as those of business ethics, political choice, economic security, quality of life, cultural development, and family planning.

Really new situations, especially in the realm of social justice, call for creative responses. We know that the Spirit moves among all the People of God, prompting them according to their particular gifts and offices, to discern anew the signs of the times and to interpret them boldly in light of the Gospel. Lay women and men are in a unique position to offer this service.

Just as by divine institution bishops, priests, and deacons have been given through ordination authority to exercise leadership as servants of God's people, so through baptism and confirmation lay men and women have been given rights and responsibilities to participate in the mission of the Church. In those areas of life in which they are uniquely present and within which they have special competency because of their particular talents, education, and experience, they are an extension of the Church's redeeming presence in the world. Recognition of lay rights and responsibilities should not create a divisiveness between clergy and laity but should express the full range of the influence of the People of God. We see this and affirm it.

MINISTRY IN THE CHURCH

As sharers in the role of Christ the Priest, the Prophet, and the King, the laity have an active part to play in the life and activity of the Church. (*Decree on the Apostolate of the Laity,* #10)

Since the Second Vatican Council new opportunities have developed for lay men and women to serve in the Church. We acknowledge gratefully the continuing and increasing contributions of volunteers and part-time workers who serve on parish and diocesan councils, boards of education, and financial, liturgical, and ecumenical committees, as well as those who exercise roles such as special minister of the Eucharist, catechist, and pastoral assistant. We are grateful, too, for the large numbers of lay people who have volunteered and are serving in the missions.

Growing numbers of lay women and men are also preparing themselves professionally to work in the Church. In this regard religious sisters and brothers have shown the way with their initiative and creativity.

Ecclesial ministers, i.e., lay persons who have prepared for professional ministry in the Church, represent a new development. We welcome this as a gift to the Church. There are also persons who serve the Church by the witness of their lives and their self-sacrificing service and empowerment of the poor in works such as administration, housing, job development, and education. All these lay ministers are undertaking roles which are not yet clearly spelled out and which are already demanding sacrifices and risks of them and their families. As lay persons increasingly engage in ecclesial ministry, we recognize and accept the responsibility of working out practical difficulties such as the availability of positions, the number of qualified applicants, procedures for hiring, just wages, and benefits.

Special mention must be made of women who in the past have not always been allowed to take their proper role in the Church's ministry. We see the need for an increased role for women in the ministries of the Church to the extent possible. We recognize the tensions and misunderstandings which arise on this question, but we wish to face these as part of a sincere attempt to become true communities of faith.

The combination of all these responses to the challenges of our time proclaims the interrelated oneness of ministry as a gift of the Spirit, and we rejoice in this.

THE CALL TO COMMUNITY

For from the wedlock of Christians there comes the family, in which new citizens of human society are born. By the grace of the Holy Spirit received in baptism these are made children of God, thus perpetuating the People of God through the centuries. The family is, so to speak, the domestic Church. (*Lumen Gentium*, #11)

Most lay persons have a primary identification with family. This influences their expectations of and contributions to the Church as the People of God. The family, as a way of life, is often taken as a model for the Church. In most families life is interdependent. Ideally, strengths and weaknesses are blended so that a growthful atmosphere is maintained.

And yet we must frankly admit that failure occurs, that in many families the ideal is not reached. For example, divorce and neglect are realities. The parish has a vital contribution to make to all families struggling to be faith communities, for the parish can serve as a model and resource for families.

Because lay women and men do experience intimacy, support, acceptance, and availability in family life, they seek the same in their Christian communities. This is leading to a review of parish size, organization, priorities, and identity. It has already led to intentional communities, basic

Christian communities, and some revitalized parish communities.

It is likely that this family characteristic of the laity will continue to influence and shape the community life of Christians. If it does, this should enable the clergy to give the kind of overall leadership which their office requires. Such trends are welcome in the Church.

CONCLUSION

The Church is to be a sign of God's Kingdom in the world. The authenticity of that sign depends on all the people: laity, religious, deacons, priests, and bishops. Unless we truly live as the People of God, we will not be much of a sign to ourselves or the world.

We are convinced that the laity are making an indispensable contribution to the experience of the People of God and that the full import of their contribution is still in a beginning form in the post-Vatican II Church. We have spoken in order to listen. It is not our intention rigidly to define or control, to sketch misleading dreams or bestow false praise. We bishops wish simply to take our place and exercise our role among the people of God. We now await the next word.